A Faculty Guide
Advising and Supervising
Graduate Students

This practical guide provides college and university faculty with resources for supervising and advising graduate assistants, guiding doctoral students through the dissertation process, and preparing the next generation of scholars. Exploring common situations that faculty and their graduate students encounter, this book provides the theoretical foundation and best practices for faculty to improve their advising and supervising practices.

Coverage includes:

- Working with part-time, online, doctoral, and master's students
- Supervising assistantships, fellowships, internships, practicums, and residencies
- Chairing dissertations and theses
- Preparing students for conferences and presentations.

Darla J. Twale has coordinated higher education leadership programs, taught for over twenty-five years, advised graduate students, and chaired numerous dissertations. She is an Adjunct Professor at the University of Pittsburgh, USA.

A Faculty Guide to Advising and Supervising Graduate Students

Darla J. Twale

Routledge
Taylor & Francis Group

NEW YORK AND LONDON

First published 2015
by Routledge
711 Third Avenue, New York, NY 10017

and by Routledge
2 Park Square, Milton Park, Abingdon, Oxon, OX14 4RN

Routledge is an imprint of the Taylor & Francis Group, an informa business

Library of Congress Cataloging in Publication Data
A catalog record for this book has been requested

ISBN: 978-1-138-80168-4 (hbk)
ISBN: 978-1-138-80169-1 (pbk)
ISBN: 978-1-315-75472-7 (ebk)

Typeset in Perpetua and Bell Gothic
by Florence Production Ltd, Stoodleigh, Devon, UK

Printed and bound in the United States of America by Publishers Graphics,
LLC on sustainably sourced paper.

To all my doctoral students whose dissertations I chaired,
with whom I presented at professional conferences and
co-authored scholarly articles and book chapters—

Thank you for enhancing my career in immeasurable ways.

And for His glory

Contents

Preface

Barely out of graduate school, I accepted a first tenure track position at Auburn University in Alabama in their Educational Leadership program. While I had been prepared to teach through pedagogical training during my undergraduate years and learned to conduct research through my master's and doctoral programs, neither place offered a whisper as to what to expect with regard to advising or supervising the graduate students assigned to me. The only entre I had to advising came through observations of *my* faculty advisors or TA supervisors. Unfortunately, I neglected to take copious notes as to *how* I was being advised or supervised and failed to tuck that information away for future use.

Winston Churchill's statement, "a riddle wrapped in a mystery inside an enigma" sums up graduate advising. It became one of the many on-the-job training opportunities faculty assumes once in a tenure track position. Faculty also inherits graduate students from colleagues, which poses an additional set of challenges. While previous generations of faculty advised a rather homogeneous population of graduate students, the current applicant pool overflows with students representing both genders, all races, age cohorts, and ethnicities, alternative lifestyles, and foreign countries who attend full or part time, in person and/or online, and plan to be teachers, researchers, and/or practitioners. These changes pose myriad challenges to effective faculty advising. What's worse, little or no help exists to aid graduate faculty advisors/supervisors in the process.

Faculty must want to become effective advisors. Good advising does not just happen and it does not happen overnight. The learning curve is steep. Unfortunately, trial and error prevail in advising/supervising until the faculty advisor/supervisor muddles through the administrative process and its obligations and becomes acquainted with the student and his/her specific goals.

Knowledge of the heterogeneous makeup of our incoming graduate student body seems paramount to effective advising. However, faculty and administration must first acknowledge the advising role as a significant aspect of the faculty position. Furthermore, they should endeavor to draw the best possible outcomes from it, that is, produce subsequent generations of effective teachers, productive scholars, and able practitioners.

At the graduate level, students should be treated as individuals rather than subjected to cookie cutter approaches. Mutual respect and trust should be evident between faculty advisor/supervisor and advisee/supervisee. As such, the advising process while becoming more time consuming for the faculty member can also develop and mature into something *more* than just a faculty/student advising relationship. The fruits of *these* types of connections can result in mentoring, collaborative research opportunities, co-presentations at conferences, co-authorships on scholarly publications, and lasting friendships.

If one were to ask graduate students from various professions and disciplines about the quality of graduate advising, student responses would span the continuum from very helpful and attentive to terribly unapproachable and intimidating. In fact, advisor/advisor relationships have been linked to student disengagement and eventual departure, so it makes sense to find ways to improve faculty advising. But academics in general have done little in this regard. Advising should not remain a mystery that we each have to solve on our own, without sharing the clues with our colleagues.

One way to assist faculty with graduate student advising tasks can be through advising guides like this one designed to cover all aspects of the graduate student process from student admission to dissertation/thesis defense and into the professional arena. Each chapter focuses on a different aspect of that process offering short vignettes of advising situations, suggestions from the scholarly literature, best practices, and resources potentially helpful to the advisor. The book opens with a chapter on the high graduate student departure rate and links it to poor faculty advising as one of the causes. In this first chapter I distinguish between mentoring and advising and focus on the latter as there are many texts on the market that deal with mentoring.

Chapter 2 follows with the graduate admissions process where the advising relationship begins. Chapter 3 focuses on the faculty/student relationship and the critical need for laying a strong and supportive foundation for advising. I devote Chapter 4 to aspects of master's and doctoral advising from entry through candidacy. Within Chapter 5, I highlight the advising needs of numerous heterogeneous student groups that now make up the graduate student body. Faculty supervision of teaching, research, or graduate student assistantships, fellowships, internships, practicums, or residencies is addressed in Chapter 6. With the rise in online graduate programs, the advisor role becomes more critical as advising from a distance poses challenges that are included in Chapter 7.

Issues related to chairing master's theses and doctoral dissertations can be found in Chapter 8. Faculty advisors are responsible for guiding students through degree and professional rites of passage. Preparing students for comprehensive written and oral examinations and defenses, co-presentation of research or scholarly work at professional conferences, and co-authorships on published works can be found in Chapter 9. In the closing chapter, I summarize the best practices covered in the previous chapters to offer suggestions to faculty advising and supervising graduate students that reflect changes in the instructional delivery of graduate education as well as changes in the student body.

Preparing the next generation of scholars and practitioners at the graduate level has largely been an individualized process. Faculty advisor meets one-on-one with his/her student in closed sessions. Little monitoring or evaluating of the content or outcome of those sessions takes place formally or informally. Consequently, the outcomes can be as productive as they are confusing. Perhaps with some assistance, more advising sessions will be constructive and establish a strong working rapport between advisor and advisee that not only spans the time in the program but also continues after graduation.

Numerous changes in higher education, student demographics, and the persistent high student departure rate necessitate guidance for faculty. These continue to challenge and confound advisors especially new ones. Texts like this one should encourage a demystification of graduate student advising. Faculty should see the possibilities in establishing strong professional relationships with their graduate students by viewing the advising, supervising, and chairing role as a significant feature of their career. Preparing our future scholars and practitioners in their field should be reason enough to provide the best advising and supervision possible.

Darla J. Twale
August 2014

What advice you have offered to one without wisdom!
And what great insight you have displayed!

Job 26: 3

Chapter 1

Retaining Graduate Students

The Critical Role of Faculty Advising

Historically, graduate education began with little organization or clear guidelines causing 1920s graduate student drop-out rates to be high. Competitive universities established processes to ensure quality graduate student entrants as early as the 1940s and also addressed the need for quality faculty to mentor them (Geiger, 2007). However, Robert Hutchins argued that quality faculty presence does not guarantee that quality students emerge "educated or advised well in the process" (Hofstadter & Smith, 1961, p. 933). Hutchins explained that professors "are bringing up their successors in the way they were brought up, so that the next crop will have the habits they have had themselves" (Hofstadter & Smith, 1961, p. 939). Some of those habits will be exemplary. Unfortunately, other habits may contribute to persistently high graduate student attrition rates (Main, 2014).

The attrition rate among doctoral students continues to be high in the 21st century (Smith, Maroney, Nelson, Abel, & Abel, 2006). Retention rates for those studying for academic and professional doctoral degrees struggle to surpass 50% (Ampaw & Jaeger, 2012; Bowen & Rudenstine, 1992; Nettles & Millett, 2006). Bowen and Rudenstine also noted the length of time to degree completion has lengthened. Proportionately, smaller PhD programs graduate more students than the larger programs, because often in larger programs, students may not benefit from individual faculty attention as is typical of the smaller programs.

Lovitts (2001) found that among the top academic reasons for student departure is student dissatisfaction with the academic programs, the faculty in general, and their advisor in particular (see also Adams, 1986, 1993). Not all students acquire the guidance they need from faculty supervisors (Perna & Hudgins, 1996). Ampaw and Jaeger (2012) noted that part-time students have less frequent access to faculty. Teaching assistantships often provided that interface with faculty that students needed, but ironically, it did not guarantee speedy graduations (Bowen & Rudenstine, 1992; Nettles & Millett, 2006). To complicate matters further, persistence and retention statistics fluctuate when considering gender, race, discipline/field, and citizenship (Ampaw & Jaeger, 2012 ; Nettles & Millett, 2006).

Retention makes reference to institutional efforts to decrease disengagement and departure rates of enrolled students. Research on institutional retention efforts over the last several decades abounds but it offers multiple reasons and conflicting results as to why master's and especially doctoral students fail to complete their degrees in a timely fashion. Institutional efforts to increase retention abound also, and vary from graduate program to graduate program. Some retention efforts work well while other efforts produce few positive results over time.

Persistence refers to students' decisions to continue to enroll beyond their matriculating semester. Persistence and non-persistence varies as the diversity among the student population increases. Looking at either side of the retention/persistence coin raises myriad issues as to why students decide to stop or drop out of their programs and what universities in general and individual programs and their faculty in particular do or neglect to do to maintain or increase student enrollment.

RETENTION IN ONLINE PROGRAMS

Changes in traditional instructional delivery to include online learning in blended, synchronous, or asynchronous formats add more variables to the retention/persistence puzzle. Increases in online enrollments resulted in equally high departure rates in these programs (Poellhuber, Roy, & Anderson, 2011). Additional issues may exist at competitive for-profit institutions versus traditional not-for-profit universities. Carroll, Ng, and Birch (2013) noted situational, organizational, and dispositional factors for non-persistence, particularly, the lack of campus-wide student support systems.

While student departure rates in online programs tend to exceed that of traditional programs, reasons fueling departure tend to be similar to traditional programs with the obvious addition of student isolation from regular human contact (Meyer, Bruwelheide, & Poulin, 2009). Meyer et al (2009) explained the unusually high student persistence rate in their online library media certificate program could be attributed to quick response time from faculty beginning at the recruitment phase and continuing throughout the program. Students attributed persistence to very timely response rates from faculty and their informal contact with their peers. The researchers concluded that "the nature of relationships with faculty, the quality of the educational experience, and [students'] own personal and individual reasons and motivations [kept] them enrolled" (Meyer et al, 2009, p. 136). Furthermore, students appreciated faculty authenticity in their communications. Students recognized the significance of the care and concern faculty had for their well-being (see also Lovitts, 1996, 2001; Lovitts & Nelson, 2000).

EFFECT OF THE FACULTY ADVISOR ON STUDENT PERSISTENCE

Myriad reasons explain student non-persistence. Ineffective institutional retention programs and student services fail to combat attrition. However, there may be one area that affects graduate student persistence more than any other and that is students' relationship with the faculty in their program. One common denominator among master's and doctoral students is their interaction with faculty in general, and their assigned or self-selected faculty advisor in particular. The faculty teaching in classrooms or online may serve as worthy role models to students, but the advising role extends beyond that. For instance, when students pursue application to a graduate program, they come into contact with faculty perhaps on the phone or via email prior to admission, and especially in person, if an interview is requested or required. Furthermore, a student's plan of study can only be done in conjunction with a faculty advisor. Assistantships and other apprenticeships require faculty supervision and guidance. Comprehensive examinations, written or oral, necessitate faculty input. Thesis and dissertation chairs and committee members come from among the faculty and guide the student's progress. Final defenses require these faculty members to sign off before the student can graduate.

Therefore, the importance of the faculty advisor in a student's graduate career cannot be underestimated. Herzig (2004) found that supportive advisors contribute to student persistence. Varying levels of support for students particularly female and minority students hindered their progress, especially when there were few female faculty members in the program. As a result, Herzig found guidance and advising to be inadequate and/or inconsistent.

For the purposes of this book, I assume that the most significant ingredient in the student's program *is* the faculty members who serve in these roles. Given that faculty advisors stand as gatekeepers to a student's future career in their profession, faculty skills and abilities, dedication and commitment to quality, and interface with the student can affect the eventual outcome (Herzig, 2004; Weidman, Twale, & Stein, 2001). Because the graduate experience tends to be more individualistic than the undergraduate experience, graduate faculty advisors while maintaining a certain style or level of quality may interact with each of their students in slightly different ways and their style may evolve over time. Meeting student needs and supervising research interests will vary by student. Therefore, graduate advising/supervising has not been a one-size-fits-all, quantifiable proposition, thus rendering it difficult to study and understand. Furthermore, supervising graduate assistants requires a different approach than student advising or overseeing thesis/dissertation research. Multiple faculty advising *and* supervising skill sets will be needed.

Richardson, Becker, Frank, and Sokol (1997) attributed student departure to neglect, mistreatment, or unwillingness of faculty to assist students. Damrosch (1995) attributed departure to either poor students unable to thrive or good students dissatisfied with their program. Lovitts (1996) regarded attrition as a necessary gatekeeping function. While these studies explain in part why the attrition still hovers at 50% among doctoral programs, some students with less effective advisors finish in spite of poor advising and some students assigned to good advisors drop out nonetheless. Graduate education may suffer as a result of a structure that favors a close relationship with only one or two faculty scholars. In the absence of more definitive data on specific advisors, the effects of various retention efforts on student persistence cannot be fully explicated (Lovitts, 1996). This explains further why the role of faculty advisor remains clouded and complicated.

ADVISING AND ATTRITION

Golde (1994) noticed a negative, though common, albeit political graduate practice: "vigorously sorting out students once they have begun their doctoral studies" (p. 21). As such, this may result in the better students getting the seasoned, more accomplished faculty advisors and the other students assigned to newer faculty or less effective advisors placing some students at a decided disadvantage.

Attrition usually follows a student's inability to connect socially and academically to their program. In Golde's (2000) study of doctoral students, she examined each student's integration into their program and their candid departure from it. Despite some degree of a collegial relationship, problems with the advisor at some point colored the relationships with the advisee. Inability to recover and find a better fit devastated these students. Disagreements with dissertation topic choices, lack of communication, direction, and support from an advisor, lack of intervention or support from department faculty or administrators signaled student need to reassess continuation in the program. Without a strong department connection, especially with the faculty advisor, the student seemed more likely to disconnect for what he/she would consider greener pastures.

Lovitts' (2001) students recounted bad experiences with faculty. They chronicled instances of misinformation, counterproductive advice, and poor TA experiences. Students noted, however, that assigned advisors were more detrimental than the self-selection of advisors, particularly when students based it on similar faculty and student research interests. Continued contact with the advisors after self-identification led to a greater chance of program completion.

Furthermore, those advisors who expressed interest in and gave of their time, students regarded as better advisors. Providing students with intellectual support, offering genuine interest in their research topic, and directing an original piece of scholarly work aligned with each other's mutual interests contributed to subsequent degree completion. In addition, to be involved with faculty outside the classroom in a professional, scholarly collaboration also portends student success in their program and enhances student professionalization (Lovitts, 2001; see also Cahn, 1994). Nyquist (2002) acknowledged that inconsistent and inappropriate supervision within the PhD program affected retention.

Smart (1987) concluded that "faculty encouragement and support to the personal and professional growth of graduate students" (p. 221) were necessary. Golde (2005) revealed that peer isolation and lack of faculty support hastened student departure. Pearson, Cowan, and Liston (2009) indicated that faculty advising remains out of touch with reality. While faculty strives to professionalize their advisees in the discipline/field, they may be overlooking the need to apprise students of the demands of the field into which they will soon enter. Faculty should encourage students to undertake cutting-edge research and make a scholarly contribution to their field/discipline not simply reinvent the wheel. Pearson et al (2009) found that faculty who allowed advisees to carry out a research project of minor significance left their programs unfulfilled.

ADMINISTRATIVE AND INSTITUTIONAL RETENTION STRATEGIES

Departing students often fail to air their concerns to their faculty advisor or the department chair before they leave. Even with better administrative criteria and screening, Lovitts (1996) hypothesized that departure could also result from institutional reasons even though university administrations tend to attribute departure to student maladaptation, financial issues, and academic concerns. Juniper, Walsh, Richardson, and Morley (2012) concluded that underlying conflicts with one's advisor/supervisor masked other critical problems. Consequently, administrators failed to explore if issues related to faculty advising/supervising might actually be *why* students depart. It would not be out of the question for attrition victims to ascribe their departure decision to personal reasons. Unfortunately, those reasons might indirectly result from institutionally rooted issues that never seek remedy.

Self-blame typical of attribution theory often prevents students from considering other factors or from expressing concerns to their faculty advisors or supervisors before departing (Lovitts, 2001). Golde (1994) concluded that students avoid verbalizing their problems with faculty advisors and academic administrators and choose instead to depart silently. Golde's (2000) study participants failed to truthfully disclose their reasons for leaving.

Failure to balance the academic and social aspects of doctoral study, integrate into the department's academic community, and internalize the normative standards of the profession often hastens student dissatisfaction that could lead to

5

departure (Golde, 2000; Lovitts, 2001). To ensure success at navigating the social and academic aspects of their program, graduate students need multiple navigation maps: one of the local departmental terrain, one of the larger professional landscape, and one outlining the role of the faculty advisor/supervisor.

ADVISING AS A RETENTION STRATEGY

Graduate schools prepare students formally for important roles they will face in their careers. Unfortunately, advising future graduate students is not one of them. Unfortunately graduate students preparing for the academic role in particular receive formal information on researching, somewhat less information on teaching, and little or no formal information on advising students (Austin, 2002). As a result, institutions can expect both good and ineffective information on advising to be transmitted.

Effective faculty advising/supervising socializes graduate students into the department and university organizational culture. Unfortunately, faculty receives little or no formal training to fulfill these advisement or supervisory roles. Faculty may be advising students in ways not aligned with demographic changes, technological advances, or entrepreneurial realities (Tierney, 1997; Weidman et al, 2001). The addition of diverse student populations, increasing information and new technologies, declining resources, accountability, and changes within academic units affects advising (Hyatt & Williams, 2011). Consequently, faculty mirror the qualities of *their* advisors and supervisors irrespective of how those particular attributes relate to the needs of entering students; the characteristics of the technologically evolving classroom or laboratory; or the dynamics of the university organizational, online, or corporate culture. Advances in communication designed to keep people connected can be adapted for faculty/student use such as social media and online interaction but generational differences between faculty and advisees/supervisees may hinder new uses of technology in forming stronger advisor/advisee or supervisor/supervisee relationships.

Sweitzer (2009) raised the issue of how closely graduate programs and departments *prioritize* faculty advising and its relationship to retention. Ultimately, teaching and research take priority among faculty time commitments and institutional reward structures in research universities. This offers little time for faculty advising let alone *exemplary* faculty advising. One explanation is that at the graduate level, students possess savvy. Faculty may believe students can maneuver through their program with minimal guidance. Sanford (1962) discussed two schools of thought: (a) applicants for graduate level work are mature and prepared for graduate study at matriculation and thus would not need to be under the constant purview of the professor; and (b) no matter what the student's developmental level at entry, he/she would eventually reach where he/she needs to be by the end of the program as a result of *all* the experiences provided in the program.

In other words, students would eventually *catch on* and if they did not, then their departure was probably *for the best*. It seemed to be a natural aspect of the gatekeeping and sorting and selecting processes needed prior to entry into the profession (Herzig, 2004; Weidman et al, 2001).

Poor or ineffective advising may stem from the faculty's lack of information on the advising role. While much has been offered to *undergraduate* faculty advisors to assist them with advising duties as well as help them to be better mentors to students, the graduate faculty member, with a decidedly more difficult task, has few if any how-to or advising-for-dummies manuals to illuminate their way. Ironically those who teach in graduate level only programs tend to be assigned graduate students. New assistant professors still recalling their own dissertation defenses are now asked to advise graduate students in programs they simultaneously have to learn about and acclimate to often on their own. Faculty is also asked to supervise graduate assistants. Assistant professors who receive graduate faculty status before tenure are tasked with overseeing thesis and dissertation research. Few if any new faculty has experience beyond their own dissertation committee experience. Administration thrusts them into an advisory/supervisory role with little regard to their own preparation or the effects this may have on the master's or doctoral student, the program retention rate, or their own tenure quest.

Much graduate faculty effort goes into graduate student recruitment and admission especially at the doctoral level. The repercussions of low graduate student persistence rates and why they may occur, affect programs and faculty efforts. High graduate student attrition rates also affect recruitment efforts, admission numbers, faculty advising and teaching loads, and faculty research efforts. Because of the time students spend in the program, whether the student has a teaching or research assistantship affects faculty time and research productivity. Ultimately, poor return on investment as a result of student attrition will be felt not only by the faculty and the department, but also by the profession (Ampaw & Jaeger, 2012). Departure harbors an implicit need for better retention strategies at the program, department, school, and university level.

RITES OF PASSAGE AND FACULTY ADVISING

The faculty/student relationship is critically related to degree completion. Lovitts (2001) determined, however, that students interact all too infrequently with faculty. Some students expected faculty to initiate contact with them. The inability of faculty to comply indicated to students that professors must be unsupportive, intimidating, and/or uncaring. Busy with their own research and teaching, faculty expected students to contact them at key junctures in their graduate program. The inability of students to comply indicated to faculty that students may not be serious about completing the program. As a result, interaction occurred less often than academic contact. Overcoming misunderstandings between faculty and students may go hand in hand with knowledge of the advising and advisee roles. The more positive the faculty/student relationship, the greater the chance students would complete their program.

Because graduate education occurs in distinct stages such as coursework, comprehensives, research proposal development, and thesis/dissertation defense, retention rates can differ at each stage. Most student departures tended to occur before the ABD (all but dissertation) status while additional opportunity for departure occurs after students reached ABD or candidacy (Bair & Haworth, 1999). What happens at these various stages can be linked to faculty advising workload and time for student interface. In fact, the student choice process to stay occurs three distinct times for thesis/dissertation students. Ampaw and Jaeger (2012) postulated that from a human capital and cost/benefit perspective, students assess the benefits they accrue at each juncture as well as the financial and emotional costs they anticipate *before* deciding to move forward with the next stage in their program or depart. How faculty advising links these statistics needs further research.

Ampaw and Jaeger (2012) found that student/faculty advising ratios negatively affected persistence in terms of the transition from coursework completion to candidacy. Faculty advising workload and committee chair assignment limits may need to be adjusted as a retention strategy to facilitate greater faculty/student interaction at this critical point. Opportunities for interaction increase for research and teaching assistants who spend more time with faculty as well as having more opportunities to increase networking and conference exposure. Graduate students without these opportunities may be less advantaged but these opportunities should not be considered a substitute for good faculty advising in the graduate program.

To complicate our understanding further, Ampaw and Jaeger (2012) learned that students of color attributed persistence to developing a more meaningful faculty advisor/advisee relationship. However, when these students formulated their research topics and proposals prior to achieving candidacy, they experienced difficulties. The researchers speculated that students of color may experience dissonance, feeling an obligation to align their research topic with their cultural identity. Faculty advisors may not be in a position to assist them effectively and thus jeopardize the students' continuance in the degree program.

Gardner's (2008) research highlighted the importance of the faculty advisor. Sufficient interaction with faculty, especially the advisor, she deemed crucial to success. Overwhelmed by new found isolation and independence during the candidacy phase, PhD students often reassess their relationship with faculty, contemplating a change in faculty advisor or topic. The isolation following coursework often decreases chances for sustained interaction with faculty as well as peers even though advances in technology can address this shortcoming. At this

8

point in their program, students must balance their need for advisor support with their desire to move toward independent scholar. Often students are ill prepared to do this and faculty thesis/dissertation chairs may not possess the skills to help them adjust to the change.

DISTINGUISHING ADVISING FROM MENTORING

According to a study by Titus and Ballou (2013), graduate faculty advising activities differ from mentoring activities in subtle ways. Advising includes chairing student dissertations, choosing classes, co-authoring and presenting papers to gain field visibility, monitoring student progress, deciding upon research topics, and providing feedback to measure student progress. While mentors may perform some of these duties, they do not perform all of them, therefore the terms *advisor* and *mentor* should not be used interchangeably or cavalierly. Not surprisingly, faculty respondents in the Titus and Ballou study recognized blurred lines between the two roles. As a result, students and faculty experienced different expectations in meeting their desired outcomes when these roles were perceived by either party to be one in the same. This may prove more problematic depending upon the degree program in terms of where faculty places emphasis and contrary wise, what students expect from the advisor versus the mentor. For example, Nettles and Millett (2006) found that students who had mentors reported strong positive faculty/student academic and social interaction and greater satisfaction with their doctoral program. While this situation was seen specifically by future academics, doctoral students preparing for careers in other non-academic roles or professional fields failed to witness it.

As distinguished from advising, mentoring tends to be a more dynamic, positive, informal role that extends beyond the prescribed role of faculty advisor and encompasses a more psychosocial and emotional dimension. While the advisor may be assigned at entry, the mentor is sought after and self-selected during the program (Schlosser, Knox, Moskowitz, & Hill, 2003; Schlosser, Lyons, Talleyrand, Kim, & Johnson, 2011).

Administratively, advising is considered obligatory and part of the faculty workload. Mentoring tends to be more voluntary and decided upon by the potential mentor and mentee, not an obligatory function of the faculty advising role or compensated workload. Not all students will have a mentor and not all faculty attempts to mentor to any or all their graduate students. A faculty/student relationship that begins as an assigned advising situation may naturally blossom into a mutually productive mentoring relationship. In addition, students may purposively seek out an advisor whom they hope will become a mentor (Schlosser et al, 2003; Schlosser et al, 2011).

Among medical residents for instance, advisors and mentors differ considerably. Advisors are residency planners/organizers, evaluators, time managers, and problem-solvers who tend to display a more administrative role set. By contrast, mentors served as career guides, advocates, and collaborators. Because the advisor role is more administrative in nature, faculty advisors needed guidelines and policies, administrative support, virtual tools, and program checklists to manage students more effectively (Woods, Burgess, Kaminetzky, McNeill, Pinheiro, & Heflin, 2010).

Volumes of scholarly literature exist on mentoring but fewer exist on advising. By contrast, little exists to address the obligations associated with the graduate faculty advising role given its potential connection to graduate program retention/attrition (Braxton, Proper, & Bayer, 2011). If faculty/student relationships remain part of the graduate student departure puzzle, examining facets of the faculty role and expectations for the advising relationship signal hope for a solution (Golde, 2000).

This faculty guide is designed to decrease the mystery of graduate student advising. The focus of the rest of this book revolves around enhancing the faculty advisor role beginning with student admission, through the first stage of the graduate program, including supervision of graduate assistants. Chapters focus on chairing of the thesis/dissertation, continuing interaction through the candidacy stage and defense to facilitating student exposure to the profession. Space specifically addressing ways for faculty to connect with a diverse population of graduate students in traditional and online formats may increase retention efforts. While each chapter suggests ways faculty can advise or supervise graduate students, the final chapter offers a summary. Perhaps the place to initiate good faculty advising begins at the beginning with the recruitment and admission of graduate students.

REFERENCES

Adams, H. (1986). *Minority participation in graduate education: An action plan.* Report of the National Invitational Forum on the Status of Minority Participation in Graduate Education. Washington, DC. (ERIC Document Reproduction Service No. ED291 272)

Adams, H. (1993). *Focusing on the campus milieu: A guide for enhancing the graduate school climate.* Notre Dame University: National Center for the Graduation of Minorities. (ERIC Document Reproduction Service No. ED381 065)

Ampaw, F., & Jaeger, A. (2012). Completing the three stages of doctoral education: An event history analysis. *Research in Higher Education, 53,* 640–660.

Austin, A. (2002). Preparing the next generation of faculty: Graduate school as socialization to the academic career. *Journal of Higher Education, 73,* 94–122.

Bair, C., & Haworth, J. (1999, November). *Doctoral student attrition and persistence: A meta-synthesis of research.* Paper presented at the annual meeting of the Association for the Study of Higher Education, San Antonio, TX. (ERIC Document Reproduction Service No. ED437 008)

Bowen, H., & Rudenstine, N. (1992). *In pursuit of the PhD*. Princeton, NJ: Princeton University Press.

Braxton, J., Proper, E., & Bayer, A. (2011). *Professors behaving badly*. Baltimore: Johns Hopkins University Press.

Cahn, S. (1994). *Saints and scamps*. Lanham, MD: Rowman & Littlefield.

Carroll, D., Ng, E., & Birch, D. (2013). Strategies to improve retention of postgraduate business students in distance learning courses: An Australian case. *Turkish Journal of Distance Education, 14*, 140–153.

Damrosch, D. (1995). *We scholars: Changing the culture of the university*. Cambridge, MA: Harvard University Press.

Gardner, S. (2008). "What's too much and what's too little?": The process of becoming an independent researcher in doctoral education. *Journal of Higher Education, 79*, 326–350.

Geiger, R. (2007). Research, graduate education, and the ecology of American universities: An interpretive history. In H. Wechsler, L. Goodchild, & L. Eisenmann (Eds.), *The history of higher of education* (3rd ed.), (pp. 316–331). ASHE Reader series. Boston: Pearson Custom Publishing.

Golde, C. (1994, November). *Student description of the doctoral student attrition process*. Paper presented at the annual meeting of the Association for the Study of Higher Education, Tucson. (ERIC Document Reproduction Service No. ED375 733)

Golde, C. (2000). Should I stay or should I go? Student descriptions of the doctoral attrition process. *Review of Higher Education, 23*, 199–227.

Golde, C. (2005). The role of the department and discipline in doctoral student attrition: Lessons from four departments. *Journal of Higher Education, 76*, 669–701.

Herzig, A. (2004). Becoming mathematicians: Women and students of color choosing and leaving doctoral mathematics. *Review of Educational Research, 72*, 171–214.

Hofstadter, R., & Smith, W. (Eds.) (1961). *American higher education: A documentary history*. Vol. II. Chicago: University of Chicago Press.

Hyatt, L., & Williams, P. (2011). 21st Century competencies for doctoral leadership faculty. *Innovative Higher Education, 36*, 53–66.

Juniper, B., Walsh, E., Richardson, A., & Morley, B. (2012). A new approach to evaluating the well-being of PhD students. *Assessment and Evaluation in Higher Education, 37*, 563–576.

Lovitts, B. (1996, April). *Who is responsible for graduate student attrition—The individual or the institution? Toward an experience of the higher and persistence rate of attrition*. Paper presented at the annual meeting of the American Education Research Association, New York. (ERIC Document Reproduction Service No. ED399 878)

Lovitts, B. (2001). *Leaving the ivory tower: The causes and consequences of departure from doctoral study*. Lanham, MD: Rowman-Littlefield.

Lovitts, B., & Nelson, C. (2000). The hidden crisis in graduate education: Attrition from PhD programs. *Academe, 86*(6), 44–50.

Main, J. (2014). Gender homophily, PhD completion, and time to degree in the humanities and humanistic social sciences. *Review of Higher Education*, *37*, 349–375.

Meyer, K., Bruwelheide, J., & Poulin, R. (2009). Why they stayed: Near perfect retention in an online certification program in library media. *Journal of Asynchronous Learning Networks*, *13*, 129–145.

Nettles, M., & Millett, C. (2006). *Three magic letters: Getting the Ph.D.* Baltimore: Johns Hopkins University Press.

Nyquist, J. (2002). The PhD: A tapestry of changes for the 21st century. *Change*, *34*(6), 12–20.

Pearson, M., Cowan, A., & Liston, A. (2009). PhD education in science. In D. Boud, & A. Lee (Eds.), *Changing practices of doctoral education* (pp. 100–112). New York: Routledge.

Perna, L., & Hudgins, C. (1996, November). *The graduate assistantship: Facilitator of graduate students' professional socialization*. Paper presented at the annual meeting of the Association for the Study of Higher Education, Memphis, TN. (ERIC Document Reproduction Service No. ED402 822)

Poellhuber, B., Roy, N., & Anderson, T. (2011). Distance students' readiness for social media and collaboration. *The International Review of Research in Open and Distance Learning*, *12*(6), 102–125.

Richardson, D., Becker, M., Frank, R., & Sokol, J. (1997). Assessing medical students' perceptions of mistreatment in their second and third years. *Academic Medicine*, *72*, 728–730.

Sanford, N. (1962). Higher education as a field of study. In N. Sanford (Ed.), *The American college* (pp. 31–73). New York: John Wiley and Sons.

Schlosser, L., Knox, S., Moskowitz, A., & Hill, C. (2003). A qualitative examination of graduate advising relationships: The advisee perspective. *Journal of Counseling Psychology*, *50*, 178–188.

Schlosser, L., Lyons, H., Talleyrand, R., Kim, B., & Johnson, W.B. (2011). Advisor–advisee relationships in graduate training programs. *Journal of Career Development*, *38*, 3–18.

Smart, J. (1987). Student satisfaction with graduate education. *Journal of College Student Personnel*, *28*, 218–222.

Smith, R., Maroney, K., Nelson, K., Abel, A., & Abel, H. (2006). Doctoral programs: Changing high rates of attrition. *Journal of Humanistic Counseling, Education, and Development*, *45*, 17–32.

Sweitzer, V. (2009). Towards a theory of doctoral student professional identity development. *Journal of Higher Education*, *80*, 1–33.

Tierney, W. (1997). Organizational socialization in higher education. *Journal of Higher Education*, *68*, 1–16.

Titus, S., & Ballou, J. (2013). Faculty members' perceptions of advising versus mentoring: Does the name matter? *Science and Engineering Ethics*, *19*, 1267–1281.

Weidman, J., Twale, D., & Stein, E. (2001). *Socialization of graduate and professional students in higher education: A perilous passage?* San Francisco: Jossey-Bass.

Woods, S., Burgess, L., Kaminetzky, C., McNeill, D., Pinheiro, S., & Heflin, M. (2010). Defining the role of advisors and mentors in post graduate medical education: Faculty perceptions, roles, responsibilities, and resource needs. *Journal of Graduate Medical Education, 2*, 195–200.

Chapter 2

Finding the Perfect Fit

Recruiting and Admitting Graduate Students

Graduate student advising should be considered by faculty advisors as a privilege rather than a service obligation. Thinking of it as obligatory with few rewards takes the challenge and the enjoyment out of advising (Barres, 2013). Instead graduate faculty advisors need to regard advising as an opportunity to identify new talent, as well as guide, develop, and introduce future colleagues to the profession. Identifying the future potential for one's profession in each year's applicant pool should be enough reason to value and appreciate the opportunity to be a part of the experience. That process begins with recruitment, application review, selection, and admission.

Madsen (2003) regarded the graduate degree as "a 'political process' because it is the faculty who determine the student's inclusion and progress toward the degree, not courses and grades" (p. 75). The recruitment, application, and selection phases offer faculty admissions committees the opportunity to determine who might be a good fit not only for the program but also for the profession. These phases permit faculty to preview students who might be a good fit for advising, supervising, and even a future mentoring relationship. Admission requirements offer faculty the chance to explore what these student hopefuls might contribute to the graduate program, the department, and the discipline. Nettles and Millett (2006) summed up the degree as "grand and desirable packaging" but they admonish faculty not to forget that "the enclosed goods *may* be highly valuable" (p. 191) so review and selection should be thorough and thoughtful. In any case, advising begins with a welcoming environment at the recruitment phase.

Reading candidate applications carefully takes time and patience. In them faculty obtains a snapshot glimpse of student fitness for the degree program. Faculty must make a decision that will be life changing for the student. As seasoned advisors, faculty knows that some of those students make it and some depart. In the latter case faculty wonder if they admitted them in error. Faculty also grapples with not admitting some students whom they speculate will not survive the rigors of a program, the coursework, or, more importantly, the research and thesis/dissertation phase. Sometimes committees reject a student based on how he/she appears to them, as if outward characteristics statistically predict subsequent performance. Speculatively, faculty admits students whose high profiles might serve to elevate the program.

Sometimes, faculty struggles with the validity of the program requirements used to predict eventual student success. Admission cycles encourage faculty to revisit the admissions criteria and determine if changes need to be discussed in order to address depth and breadth issues in the applicant pool. Applicant review time is the perfect occasion to determine with some certainty how student research dovetails with faculty agendas and how student employment interests mesh with job prospects in the field. Selecting students for traditional programs as compared to online programs presents unique challenges to admissions committees and faculty advisors that transcend disciplines as well.

Hope and Dreams

Chris was Professor Douvanis' first appointment. He worked in mid-management in the enrollment office and wanted his doctorate in educational leadership. Douvanis asked Chris why he chose this degree. Chris stated he wanted to be president of a large research university someday. Professor Douvanis posed the same question to Shane, his next appointment. Shane held a bachelor's in math and a master's in vocal performance, taught remedial math at a local community college, and directed a church choir. Shane desired to teach math and/or music at any college or university that would take him. While both men had stellar credentials and held great promise for the EdD program, Douvanis wondered about their current fit and future goals.

RECRUITMENT

Gardner, Hayes, and Neider (2007) noted the importance of recruiting students who align with the values, realities, and goals of a particular program. Promising applicants like Shane may be pursuing the wrong degree. Douvanis knew that a degree in educational leadership could be more of a detriment to Shane than a benefit. While Chris found himself in the correct department, Douvanis wondered if his goal was realistic given the common career path of research university presidents. Admitting either might be a disservice to both but Douvanis pondered the precarious nature of recruitment given their stellar credentials.

Normally, faculty looks for a "good fit" to their specialization from the pool of undergraduate or pre-professional degree programs. However, some graduate professional programs such as counseling and educational leadership offer no undergraduate degrees. Students who enter graduate programs with dissimilar undergraduate degrees come to the program at some disadvantage. This is especially evident with regard to the prevailing norms and values of that department, discipline, or field. In these instances, thorough pre-advising and orientation appears more critical. However, the diversity in background of applicants like Chris and Shane may enhance the program in myriad ways.

Faculty should not rely on voluntary candidate pools alone to supply them with students who would be good fits for their programs. These pools may include people better suited for other programs or passively exclude excellent candidates from underrepresented and international populations. Recruitment avenues should not simply reach for the low hanging fruit but cast a wider net with other four-year colleges, minority-dominated institutions, and other academic and non-academic departments on campus. Prospects may come from untapped off-campus sites such as business, industry, and multicultural service areas (Pruitt & Isaac, 1985; Quarterman, 2008; Reichert, 2006).

Woodhouse (2006) found that although departments have administrative recruitment plans, most graduate faculty reported not being asked by their chair to participate in recruitment activities. However, most faculty regarded recruitment as part of their role and therefore, nearly half of the respondents involved themselves in the recruitment process without needing administrative direction. Minority faculty and program coordinators/directors tended to be more involved in recruitment than other faculty and administrative groups.

Getting underrepresented students in the career pipeline begins with the graduate recruitment process (Juarez, 1991). Prospective students also need to be made aware in the recruitment process of the likelihood of finding a same race/same sex advisor (and mentor). If the student chooses to attend the program, the student/faculty of color ratio should be considered so as not to overtax faculty or underserve the student. Urban institutions may provide additional mentors and resources for students of color at neighboring institutions which should be explored to assist potential applicants (Grant & Simmons, 2008).

While doctoral education can be isolating, Damrosch (1995) argued that we rarely if ever factor that into the recruitment or admission screening process. Faculty rarely makes a determination as to whether a student can effectively move from the support of classroom cohorts to the isolation of the thesis/dissertation research. Graduate programs and admission committees tend not to advertise the singular cultural atmosphere of the thesis/dissertation phase to prospective students and how it differs from the coursework phase. They may offer alternatives to combat it, however, and those should factor in the recruitment process.

APPLICATION PROCESS

Education versus History

Immediately after graduating from college on a full football scholarship, Adam secured a graduate assistantship on the coaching staff of an SEC powerhouse. Now he was tasked with securing admission to a master's program on campus. With a growing interest in Renaissance history, Adam submitted his application, in person, to the history department. He encountered Professor McKeever in the suite office. Hoping to have a moment to speak to the professor about the program, Adam instead received only a brief, "Thank you, young man." Days later, a denial letter appeared in Adam's mailbox. During his search for another option, peers at the football complex recommended Foundations of Education, a graduate program that they thought might interest him. Quickly, he submitted his application. Master's admission committee coordinator, Professor Gearing read Adam's materials with utter delight. With his 1300+ GRE score, a 3.5 undergrad GPA from a Big Ten school, and a very well-written essay, Adam's credentials floated to the top of the candidate pool. History's loss was surely to be the Foundations department's and Gearing's gain.

Typical admissions criteria at the graduate level include some of the following: application form; MAT or GRE test scores; professional tests like the GMAT, MCAT or LSAT, or specific departmental exams; transcripts from undergraduate and graduate programs; multiple recommendations from academic and/or professional sources; pre-submitted and/or extemporaneous writing samples; resume or vita; statement of career aspirations and research interests; previous work experience in one's field, especially in management; and a face-to-face, phone, or virtual interview with one faculty member or a committee of faculty members in the department. Other screening items useful to the committee include honors received, Phi Beta Kappa membership, previous research, assistantship/internship placements, civic and extra-curricular experiences, leadership positions held, and up-to-date certifications (Brink, 1989; Hedlund, Wilt, Nebel, Ashford, & Sternberg, 2006; Saaty, France, & Valentine, 1991). International student applications arrive with additional items like TOEFL scores.

In other words, the normative application process includes qualitative and quantitative assessments (Hoeffer & Gould, 2000) of cognitive and non-cognitive factors (Grapczynski & Beasley, 2013; Meggenson, 2009) subjected to objective and subjective screening criteria (Pruitt & Isaac, 1985). Madsen (2003) encouraged multiple means for admission in order to determine the student's ability more holistically. Multiple diagnostic tests may also be administered to students to further ascertain their fitness and establish if students are ready for the rigors of writing or advanced mathematics and statistics needed to complete a dissertation.

Admission traditionally includes cognitive factors which are what Professor Gearing used to judge Adam's fitness for the program. However, usage remains controversial in the midst of conflicting research because standardized tests proved valid in science fields (Kuncel & Hezlett, 2007) and experimental, clinical, and counseling psychology (Purdy, Reinehr, & Swartz, 1989) but inconclusive in some of the other hard and soft disciplines (Alexandre, Portela, & Sá, 2009). In addition, the GRE was not a strong predictor of success in graduate nursing programs (Katz, Chow, Motzer, &Woods, 2009; Newton & Moore, 2006b). Hoeffer and Gould (2000) reported that business schools found standardized tests predicted full-time student outcomes while GPA/QPA predicted part-time student outcomes. Nauta (2000) suggested that psychology students underestimate or overestimate the importance of various graduate admissions criteria which could alter their chances for selection into specific programs. Clear information, preparation resources, and weighted entrance formulas should be articulated to students and helpful to faculty admissions committees.

In the absence of or in addition to standardized instruments, admissions committees can glean non-cognitive student personal and professional characteristics through multiple means such as emotional stability, conscientiousness, openness, and attitudinal factors, such as interest, motivation, self-concept, and self-efficacy. Portfolios, structured or unstructured letters of recommendation from professors and supervisors, interviews, research experience, written statements, and other field-specific means can supplement cognitive measures (Dejnozski & Smiley, 1983; Halberstam & Redstone, 2005; Meggenson, 2009). According to Dejnozski and Smiley, these offer a "value-added system" that goes beyond the quantitative to include qualitative measures that encompass multiple means of assessing the candidate.

Different disciplines and professional areas should focus on additional ways to determine candidate fitness because standardized tests and GPAs cannot account for everything that admission committees need to know about the student (Hedlund et al, 2006). For example, when psychology admissions committees examined standardized test scores and student transcripts to determine admission and found low scores, faculty decided to look for other indicators of potential success rather than to disregard the file (Landrum, 2003).

In order to determine a candidate's potential and practical intelligence to succeed in a competitive business program, for example, faculty appraised the student's skill set for solving more practical business problems (Hedlund et al, 2006).

Johnson (2000) argued for the ability to identify strong candidates for a graduate program in gifted education through the use of portfolio options to supplement the required applicant information. This portfolio contained scholarly writing, a curriculum plan, teaching materials, and/or evidence of an accomplishment outside of education. Due to the nature of the nursing program, Newton and Moore (2006b) suggested that a candidate's previous professional accomplishments would be more telling than heavy reliance on the GRE alone.

Arnold, Gonzalez, and Gaengler (2011) acknowledged that "individual student success is dependent on his [*sic*] own abilities which can be detected in the selection process, on his or her personal motivation (which can be discussed during the interview or via student counseling) and on the enthusiasm of university teachers" (p. 242). In the history department, Professor McKeever completely ignored Adam's credentials perhaps turned off by his commanding physical appearance as a football player. Faculty in that department never gave Adam an opportunity to prove his capabilities. By the same token, neither did Professor Gearing who only looked at the cognitive assessments. She assumed Adam could handle the rigors of the program but never determined through examining other non-cognitive factors if he truly *was* a good fit.

Writing intensive programs or those with a senior paper or master's thesis give admission committees better insight into a student's ability to handle the rigors of doctoral-level writing (Newton & Moore, 2006a). Newton and Moore recommended the submission of a scholarly paper. Faculty assessment of the applicant's writing skills should also lend insight into their cognitive abilities.

The use of written statements can also determine "motivation or career potential," as well as predict achievement (Hoeffer & Gould, 2000, p. 225). Written goal statements as part of the candidate folder can show depth of communication skills and critical thinking ability. Being coherent and concise, these statements can also show how well students follow directions. In addition, these statements can provide insight into the applicant's skill mastery, research interests crucial to advisor/advisee matching, and potential for professional role acceptance (Halberstam & Redstone, 2005; Newton & Moore, 2006a).

Similarly prior knowledge of and exposure to the field of pediatric psychology does not occur during undergraduate training, making it more difficult for faculty to assess candidate files. Beyond the standardized tests and GPA/QPA, faculty has few additional means to determine student fitness for the field or advisor/advisee matches (Karazsia & McMurtry, 2012), as was the case with Chris and Shane. In order to assess student fitness, faculty valued student training in research methods and evaluation as well as student work on a previous research project such as an honors thesis or conference presentation.

While cognitive assessments may predict academic performance, they offer little insight into clinical performance. Qualities such as motivation and perseverance are difficult to assess in prospective candidate files but can be determined more easily during interviews, whether unstructured, semi-structured, or structured (Brink, 1989). The interviews in the Arnold et al (2011) study of dental school hopefuls assessed "applicants' motivation, self-appraisal, maturity, and interpersonal skills" (p. 241). Be cautious, however, because faculty interviewers come with varying levels of interviewing experience in addition to particular faculty biases that necessitate attention to validity and inter-rater reliability issues.

Because quantitative assessments did not accurately predict student success in a UK dental program, Foley and Hijazi (2013) found that academic prowess in dental schools can be assessed and highly useful, but practicing dentists also need to demonstrate manual dexterity and effective communicative abilities as well as work effectively in teams. Their use of multiple mini-interviews assessed student skills and abilities and predicted future academic and professional performance. They found that multiple interviews guarded against interviewer bias when a structured assessment system was employed. Arnold et al (2011) also found that manual dexterity measures rank high in importance and thus call for more tests in circulation to evaluate these critical dexterity skills.

To gain insight into a candidate's professionalism, Grapczynski and Beasley (2013) utilized a non-cognitive profile matrix that encompassed core areas of the occupational therapy profession—"practice, leadership, education, research, and professional socialization"—in order "to identify occupational therapist program applicants who, while undergraduates, have engaged in some of the activities that indicate professional promise" (p. 113). Across the top of the matrix they included room for the activity, its duration, and how often the activity was performed by the student. While this facilitated the quantitative frequency, it did not allow for quality outcomes. In addition to the results of this matrix, faculty took into consideration GPA, letters of recommendation, professional practice experience, and the interview and writing sample. Each component in the file had a maximum number of points allotted with a minimum cut-off score expected for admission.

In a large national study of admissions' policies for graduate programs, Attiyeh and Attiyeh (1997) determined that admissions committees, in order to ensure diversity in their programs, established higher standards for mainstream groups already overrepresented in their candidate pool. Not all faculty committees will value this approach but it serves as an option.

From an administrative perspective, elaborate candidacy files increase faculty involvement in the admission process. Faculty need more time to review, score, and assess materials and clearly defined ways of evaluating students. Some folders will differ from others, complicating faculties' decision-making processes. However, the breadth and depth of information used to showcase each candidate would likely increase student diversity, better determine student potential for success, allow for clearer program–student fit, encourage better advisor/advisee matches, and affect retention (Johnson, 2000).

FACULTY SELECTION OF APPLICANTS

Admission Windfall

The applicant pool for the coming fall master's and doctoral cohorts looked promising. Professor Schaid gleamed at all those folders stacked high upon her desk. Among them were eight applications from employees located throughout the administrative and financial arm of the university. Some worked in treasury services, contracts and grants, and the budget office, while others came from the controller's office. Some applicants reported to other applicants within the system. All of them exceeded the written criteria for admission. There was a nice gender balance and nice age spread among this seasoned group. Students for both degrees would take classes together, so the only problem appeared that superiors and subordinates would likely be in the same class at the same time. On the plus side, the presence of this critical mass of financially minded students would add a wealth of experience to the graduate program. On the flip side, that might mean too many from one area in the classes might skew the discussion their way instead of encompassing broader perspectives. Those not part of their group might feel intimidated by their presence, especially those in their early twenties who just graduated from college. Professor Schaid wondered now whether she should admit everyone, advise these students herself, or divide them among her colleagues.

Admission committees should be mindful from the moment the candidate's file is reviewed that faculty and student interests should align. Professor Schaid would do well to match students with the appropriate advisor if she was not that person, even though maintaining consistency within this cohort seemed important to her. In their study of engineering students, Sutton and Sankar (2011) advocated that pairing students with faculty having the same or similar research interests increased retention. Advisor/advisee matches should consider the faculty's expertise in the topic area students wish to research as well as in supervisor/supervisee assistantship matches (Ahmad, 2007). More importantly, determining if the student's interests and abilities and background fit well with existing faculty should be as important as test scores, interviews, and writing samples. Take care at entry not to admit students whose interests do not dovetail faculty's or whom faculty believe are not yet ready for master's/doctoral-level work.

As per established admission policies and expectations for the field/discipline, the inclusion and concomitant exclusion of individuals will determine the esprit of the entering cohort of students as Professor Schaid anticipated. The interdependence of this cohort group determines student satisfaction with the program and perhaps their eventual graduation from it. They would support one another also as Professor Schaid anticipated.

Politics and Professional Courtesy

Professors Shannon, Costa, and Cho interviewed Andre for a place in the fall doctoral cohort in secondary school administration. Actually, they rejected Andre's application weeks earlier because they believed that his undergraduate and master's work, his very low GRE scores, and his writing sample placed him at a decided disadvantage for success compared to other accepted applicants. Their department chair received a call from the dean who received a call from the provost asking out of professional courtesy, if the committee would reconsider and at least grant Andre an interview. The committee learned that Andre contacted the provost's office when his denial letter arrived. So out of respect for the provost, the committee interviewed Andre. They were concerned that his extemporaneous writing sample and his test scores on both the language and math sections of the GRE indicated to them it might be difficult for him to complete the dissertation. "I don't test well so I took the GRE twice," Andre offered. Dr. Cho inquired, "Knowing you feel you do not test well, to what extent did you take advantage of test preparation materials and online sites to help you prepare?" Andre responded, "None, I didn't have time."

In the course of admission committee deliberations, faculty may realize that their policies and standards may confine the selection process. In addition, committee members might need to address their own biases in the selection/denial process (Giddens, 2010). As a result, requirements for entrance concern many minority applicants like Andre (Webb & Allen, 1994) largely due to the inconclusive nature of admission criteria on actual performance (Curtis, Lind, Plesh, & Finzen, 2007) and the conflicting research on standardized testing (Hoeffer & Gould, 2000). Therefore, if students appear promising but have deficiencies than can be remediated, offering probation or contingency admission so that students can remedy deficiencies eliminates much faculty doubt about a student's ability to succeed in the program (Brink, 1989).

Cole and Lewis (1993) recommended professional courtesy be extended when students challenge faculty's academic decision for admission. Faculty should consider credential re-review and re-interviewing, as well as asking for additional information that would support the student's case. Just conducting an interview may not provide definitive evidence that Andre would or would not succeed. Additional materials should have been requested and questions more carefully crafted by Professors Shannon, Costa, and Cho. While Andre may not have tested or interviewed well, a more complete picture of his work/work experience would have broadened the picture and more thoroughly highlighted the deficiencies in his file. Measuring the outcomes with the prevailing admission policies/criteria should provide the faculty with data and the impetus to revisit their admission

22

policies for further affirmation or contemplate new criteria for admission decisions and/or selection procedures (Giddens, 2010).

Furthermore, Davis and Moore (1972) noted that inequality prevails in the graduate admissions process. Major factors that contribute included undergraduate institution, gender, race, ethnicity, native country, and financial resources, as well as additional personal, social, and psychological issues. Some admissions policies/formulas offer incentives to underrepresented populations while others do not. Pastine and Pastine (2012) contended that offering underrepresented applicants like Andre bonus points to allow them to qualify for admission spoils their inclination to achieve on their own. Pastine and Pastine called for one rather than multiple incentive structures due to the possibility of greater attrition occurring among populations unable to perform well academically. However, another approach would be to augment the application portfolio to include multiple pieces of information that present more aspects and textures of each applicant to the committee members.

ADVISOR/ADVISEE MATCHING AND ASSIGNMENT

The applicant goal statement offers faculty a starting point when assigning initial advisors. For subsequent selection of an advisor, vitae will aid faculty in helping students select thesis/dissertation committee chairs and committee members. Periodic colloquia composed of faculty and students allows faculty to present their research interests and for students to discuss their proposal topics in order to facilitate better matches (TWIG, 1996). This can be especially important for students who enter graduate programs with dissimilar undergraduate degrees because they matriculate to the program with some disadvantage. They may not be knowledgeable of the prevailing norms and values of that department, discipline, or field. In these instances, thorough student orientation and frequent advising appears more critical for quality outcomes and retention (Smart, 1987).

Faculty and student views of and expectations for advising differ (Allen & Smith, 2008). Paramount for each group, however, is receiving accurate, timely information related to the graduate program. Austin (2002) advocated that a set of advising standards be provided to faculty when hired and to students at matriculation. Giving students an opportunity to view the future to realize what to expect as well as what is expected from them by academe is crucial. While faculty is focused on transmitting knowledge and helping students create their own, faculty often neglect to provide students with an opportunity to see into the life of the mind. Students need an open forum in which to periodically comprehend their new social and cultural environment.

Part of the information doctoral students need to receive before or upon entry is that doctoral-level education is not a continuation of undergraduate or master's schooling but a demanding purposeful pursuit of intellectual growth and development (Walker, Golde, Jones, Bueschel, & Hutchings, 2008). Perhaps some students would choose to leave if the whole sordid picture was revealed to them but it is to their advantage for faculty to show them reality (Austin, 2002) early in the program or at the interview process, so they can forge ahead accordingly (Golde, 1998).

Golde (1998) indicated that advisor/advisee mismatches became a reason for leaving, especially where "dissimilar working style and the inability to communicate" prevail (p. 58). Furthermore, faculty advising includes informing students how the institution expects the student to navigate through the system but not necessarily expecting the faculty member to take responsibility for the student's navigation (Allen & Smith, 2008).

How Not to Handle a Rejection Letter

As was school policy, students could take six credit hours as a non-admitted student pending application to the doctoral program. Austin took two courses from Professor Goldberg who also sat in on the interview. When Austin left the interview, the faculty discussed his potential fitness for the program. His test scores were marginal, his undergraduate and graduate work appeared fine, and his statement of purpose merely adequate. Dr. Goldberg noted that Austin missed four weeks of her class without explanation, did well on the midterm but handed in a very substandard term paper. The committee noted during the interview that Austin appeared nervous and fidgety and bristled on several questions posed to him. Austin offered no thought to his research direction but mumbled only a possibility. They wondered if he would be a good fit for the program as no one on faculty specialized remotely in that research area. Committee consensus was to deny Austin entry at this time. When Austin received the letter, he immediately shot off a rambling, caustic email accusing the faculty committee and the program director of collectively conspiring to ruin his future based on the ridiculous guidelines for program admission.

The probability for student success should guide the admission process because it offers faculty their first opportunity to determine the potential for success of each candidate. Unfortunately, the process remains flawed despite faculty's best efforts: Admission committees admit students who eventually drop out and contrariwise, wonder if the applicants denied admission might have walked at graduation (Brink, 1989). Reasons for the flawed nature of the admissions process could be related to the range of faculty and administrators making the decisions, the criteria they use, and/or the weighting of objective/subjective and cognitive/non-cognitive criteria. For instance, the determination of the value of an undergraduate or graduate GPA and the institution from which it was conferred can vary between faculty assessors. In addition, faculty's impression of a student drawn largely from a short interview may focus more on personality and language skills than upon a student's future potential (Brink, 1989).

Dismissals or denials for academic reasons can cause students and faculty great consternation. Program directors must adhere to explicitly stated guidelines for due process (Cole & Lewis, 1993). When professional judgment becomes the reason for student denial, the picture often blurs as Professor Goldberg learned. Professional judgment by faculty in academic matters may be more difficult to explicitly assess and explain to students like Austin. However, faculty is reminded to apply consistent principles regarding instances of professional judgment.

BEST PRACTICES

Recruitment

- View recruitment/advising as a part of the teaching load rather than part of the service expectation (Woodhouse, 2006).
- Work with enrollment management personnel on campus or an outside recruitment consultant to enhance recruitment efforts (Woodhouse, 2006).
- Encourage faculty to work with program directors/coordinators and department chairs in formulating collective recruitment plans (Woodhouse, 2006).
- Offer workshops to explain the application and admission process to minority hopefuls. This might include standardized test preparation, explanation of the application process, the interview process, and roundtable interaction with graduate faculty and current graduate students of color (Juarez, 1991).

Selection and Admission

- To score various quantitative and especially qualitative student admissions materials use a rubric and/or a weighted system to diminish subjectivity and bias from the selection process (Katz et al, 2009; Newton & Moore, 2006a; Saaty et al, 1991).
- Base faculty admission decisions on a balanced collectivity of cognitive/non-cognitive factors rather than overly weight any one of them.
- Consider offering conditional admission or allow students to take one or two courses while in the admission process (Pruitt & Isaac, 1985).
- Keep an open mind and open door to all students, even the ones for whom you do not have a personal affinity (Barres, 2013).

Advising Assignment

- To increase retention, match faculty and student on various criteria including research interests, background, gender, and race/ethnicity.

- Faculty should assess how much knowledge, time, and support/resources they have to offer a particular student in the office, lab, or conference setting (Barres, 2013).
- Departments need to monitor student progress beginning at entry and proceeding through post degree (Liechty, Schull, & Liao, 2009). Encourage faculty admissions committees to examine policies and procedures and refine and update accordingly to encourage rather than hinder student progress.

RESOURCES

- Grapczynski and Beasley's (2013) non-cognitive profile matrix provides a helpful guide to admission committees wishing to design their own.
- Visit grad.edu/index.php/faculty-and-staff/recruitment/recruitment-resources/ to get additional ideas and best practices devised by faculty at the University of Georgia (retrieved November 11, 2014).

REFERENCES

Ahmad, K. (2007). *PhD: The pursuit of excellence*. Singapore: Thompson Learning Asia.

Alexandre, F., Portela, M., & Sá, C. (2009). Admissions conditions and graduates' employability. *Studies in Higher Education, 34*, 795–805.

Allen, J., & Smith, C. (2008). Faculty and student perspectives on advising: Implications for student dissatisfaction. *Journal of College Student Development, 49*, 609–624.

Arnold, W., Gonzalez, P., & Gaengler, P. (2011). The predictive value of criteria for student admissions to dentistry. *European Journal of Dental Education, 15*, 236–243.

Attiyeh, G., & Attiyeh, R. (1997). Testing for bias in graduate school admissions. *Journal of Human Resources, 32*, 524–548.

Austin, A. (2002). Preparing the next generation of faculty: Graduate school as socialization to the academic career. *Journal of Higher Education, 73*, 94–122.

Barres, B. (2013). How to pick a graduate advisor. *Neuron, 80*, 275–279.

Brink, W. (1989). Selecting graduate students. *Journal of Higher Education, 70*, 517–523.

Cole, B., & Lewis, R. (1993). Gatekeeping through termination of unsuitable social work students: Legal issues and guidelines. *Journal of Social Work Education, 29*, 150–159.

Curtis, D., Lind, S., Plesh, O., & Finzen, F. (2007). Correlation of admission criteria with academic performance in dental students. *Journal of Dental Education, 71*, 1314–1321.

Damrosch, D. (1995). *We scholars: Changing the culture of the university*. Cambridge, MA: Harvard University Press.

Davis, K., & Moore, W. (1972). Some principles of stratification. In G. Ritzer (Ed.), *Issues, debates, and controversies: An introduction to sociology* (pp. 214–225). Boston: Allyn & Bacon.

Dejnozki, E., & Smiley, L. (1983). Selective admissions criteria in graduate teacher education programs. *Journal of Teacher Education, 34*, 24–28.

Foley, J., & Hijazi, K. (2013). The admission process in a graduate-entry dental school: Can we predict academic performance. *British Dental Journal, 214*, E4.

Gardner, S., Hayes, M., & Neider, X. (2007). The dispositions and skills of a PhD, in education: Perspectives of faculty and graduate students in one College of Education. *Innovative Higher Education, 31*, 287–299.

Giddens, J. (2010). The admissions committee: Experiential learning in an online graduate nursing education course. *Journal of Nursing Education, 49*, 175–176.

Golde, C. (1998). Beginning graduate school: Explaining first year doctoral attrition. In M. Anderson (Ed.), *The experience of being in graduate school: An exploration* (pp. 55–64). New Directions for Higher Education no. 101. Amherst, NY: Prometheus Books.

Grant, C., & Simmons, J. (2008). Narratives on experiences of African-American women in the academy: Conceptualizing effective mentoring relationships of doctoral students and faculty. *International Journal of Qualitative Studies in Education, 21*, 501–517.

Grapczynski, C., & Beasley, J. (2013). Occupational therapy admissions: Professionalization and personality. *Journal of Allied Health, 42*, 112–117.

Halberstam, B., & Redstone, F. (2005). The predictive value of admissions materials on objective and subjective measures of graduate school performance in speech-language pathology. *Journal of Higher Education Policy and Management, 27*, 261–272.

Hedlund, J., Wilt, J., Nebel, K., Ashford, S., & Sternberg, R. (2006). Assess practical intelligence in business school admissions: A supplement to the *Graduate Management Admission Test. Learning and Individual Differences, 16*(2), 101–127.

Hoeffer, P., & Gould, J. (2000). Assessment of admission criteria for predicting students' academic performance in graduate business school. *Journal of Education for Business, 75*, 225–229.

Johnson, A. (2000). Admission procedures for a graduate program: Matching practice and paradigm. *Roeper Review, 23*, 83–84.

Juarez, C. (1991). Recruiting minority students for academic careers: The role of graduate student and faculty mentors. *PS: Political Science and Politics, 24*, 530–540.

Karazsia, B., & McMurtry, M. (2012). Graduate admissions in pediatric psychology: The importance of undergraduate training. *Journal of Pediatric Psychology, 37*, 127–135.

Katz, J., Chow, C., Motzer, S., & Woods, S. (2009). The Graduate Record Examination: Help or hindrance in nursing graduate school admissions? *Journal of Professional Nursing, 25*, 369–372.

Kuncel, N., & Hezlett, S. (2007). Standardized tests predict graduate students' success. *Science, 315*(5815), 1080–1081.

Landrum, R.E. (2003). Graduate admission in psychology: Transcripts and the effect of withdrawals. *Teaching of Psychology, 30*, 323–325.

Liechty, J., Schull, C., & Liao, M. (2009). Facilitating dissertation completion and success among doctoral students in social work. *Journal of Social Work Education, 45*, 481–498.

27

Madsen, C. (2003). Instruction and supervision of graduate students in music education. *Research Studies in Education*, *21*, 72–79.

Meggenson, L. (2009). Non-cognitive constructs in graduate admissions: An integrative review of available instruments. *Nurse Educator*, *34*, 254–261.

Nauta, M. (2000). Assessing the accuracy of psychology undergraduate perceptions of graduate admission criteria. *Teaching of Psychology*, *27*, 277–280.

Nettles, M., & Millett, C. (2006). *Three magic letters: Getting the Ph.D.* Baltimore: Johns Hopkins University Press.

Newton, S., & Moore, G. (2006a). The significance of graduate admission written goal statements. *Journal of Professional Nursing*, *22*, 205–209.

Newton, S., & Moore, G. (2006b). Undergraduate grade point average and Graduate Record Exam scores: The experience of one graduate nursing program. *Nursing Education Perspectives*, *28*, 327–331.

Pastine, I., & Pastine, T. (2012). Student incentives and preferential treatment in college admissions. *Economics of Education Review*, *31*, 123–130.

Pruitt, A., & Isaac, P. (1985). Discrimination in recruitment, admission, and retention of minority graduate students. *Journal of Negro Education*, *54*, 526–536.

Purdy, J., Reinehr, R., & Swartz, J. (1989). Graduate admissions criteria of leading psychology departments. *American Psychologist*, *44*, 960–961.

Quarterman, J. (2008). An assessment of barriers and strategies for recruitment and retention of a diverse graduate student population. *College Student Journal*, *42*, 947–967.

Reichert, W. (2006). A success story: Recruiting and retaining underrepresented minority doctoral students in biomedical engineering. *Liberal Education*, *92*(3), 52–55.

Saaty, T., France, J., & Valentine, K. (1991). Modeling the graduate business school admissions process. *Socio-Economic Planning Sciences*, *25*, 155–162.

Smart, J. (1987). Student satisfaction with graduate education. *Journal of College Student Personnel*, *28*, 218–222.

Sutton, K., & Sankar, C. (2011). Student satisfaction with information provided by academic advisors. *Journal of STEM Education*, *12*(7/8), 71–86.

TWIG Writing Group. (1996). A feminist perspective on graduate student–advisor relationships. *Feminist Teacher*, *10*, 17–25.

Walker, G., Golde, C., Jones, L., Bueschel, A., & Hutchings, P. (2008). *The formation of scholars.* San Francisco: Jossey-Bass.

Webb, M., & Allen, L. (1994). Graduate business students: Factors that differentiate diverse markets' matriculating decisions. *Journal of Marketing for Higher Education*, *5*, 87–108.

Woodhouse, S. (2006). Faculty involvement in graduate student recruitment. *Journal of College Admissions*, *190*, 26–32.

Chapter 3

Laying the Foundation

Forming Strong Faculty/Student Relationships

The bond created by faculty and graduate students holds implications for the duration of their association and perhaps afterwards into professional practice. While this relationship is important from matriculation through the development of the plan of study, it becomes even more critical during the thesis/dissertation process. While this association functions to complete professional tasks, faculty must not overlook its emotional component. Faculty may need to change their relationship patterns to fulfill student needs in order to bring out the unique talents in each of their students.

Matching personalities and research interests appear to be critical to a stronger bond and to successful student *and* faculty outcomes. However, faculty also needs to relate to students as their advisors and supervisors of their research and practice. Relating merely as friends or intimate partners will be detrimental to the student and perhaps to the career of the faculty member. Gender, race, sexual orientation, citizenship, and ethnic differences add texture to the faculty/student relationship as does student status and online delivery. This chapter focuses on the faculty/student relationship as opposed to the advisor/advisee relationship, which will be discussed in the next chapter.

Nettles and Millett (2006) acknowledged that "making one solid faculty connection paves the way for a more favorable outlook on a student's other faculty interactions" (p. 191) rendering a halo effect of program satisfaction. The research on how faculty and students relate to each other and how it affects successful program/degree completion begins with the nature of the faculty role and includes the personalities of the faculty and how faculty creates a lasting bond that carries the student through the program and beyond.

Each case scenario presented in the chapter alludes to the importance of the faculty/student relationship and what it properly takes to maintain it and what should be avoided. Despite the fact that the faculty/student relationship affects student satisfaction and success, neither faculty nor student understands all facets of each other's roles and the interplay between the two and how it might affect them as their relationship evolves. Students may not have a clear expectation of the faculty role and faculty may not have a clear expectation of the student role. Understanding how each one is to perform their role with regard to role and status expectations would appear to be important in preventing role ambiguity and role conflict (Descutnes & Thelen, 1989; Rosen & Bates, 1967). Because of the importance of the faculty/student relationship to student success in graduate education, faculty and students must work in tandem not in isolation or at opposition to sustain this important dyad.

Adjusting to Role Evolution

Yesterday, Professor Norbert received a call from Patricia, a graduated student whose dissertation she chaired. Excited about a new job prospect, Patricia wanted to alert Norbert that someone wanting a reference would be calling. During the hour-long call, Patricia and Norbert caught up on things since their last conversation months earlier. The conversation drifted from family to the old department faculty to the new job prospect and back to her dissertation days. Back then, Patricia regularly phoned Norbert when she encountered issues with her data, wanted to brainstorm ideas, or talk about her upcoming defense. They told one another over the years that knowing each other greatly enriched their lives. Going to conferences and presenting together were things they would always remember. The hardest thing Norbert has had to do in the last year is to try to get Patricia to now call her Donna!

INTERPERSONAL ASPECTS OF THE FACULTY/STUDENT RELATIONSHIP

Heathcott (2007) regarded faculty's relationship to students as having greater importance in a graduate program than the curriculum. Specifically, the faculty/student relationship is the basis for career development at the graduate level. This conundrum places the faculty in a precarious relationship with the student as master to apprentice at entry, and simultaneously moving to future colleague status as the student approaches graduation. In addition, the faculty/student relationship often evolves into mentoring (Schlosser, Lyons, Talleyrand, Kim, & Johnson, 2011b). As such, faculty advisors and thesis/dissertation chairs must extend beyond their faculty position to assume roles which entail personal growth and professional development for faculty and students alike (Galbraith, 2003). As illustrated, Patricia needs to realize that her relationship with Professor Norbert evolved from student apprentice to that of respected colleague. The interpersonal dynamics changed over time to warrant the mature acceptance of the scholar role which is difficult for some students. This transition often takes time and patience.

Watching the transformation of a graduate student to independent scholar should cause advisors great pride and satisfaction enough so as to encourage investment in the relationship and its inherent transformational process. However, students need not be clones of their advisors but rather be purposefully encouraged to follow their own research interests, give life to their own research problems, and be supported when they explore their own cultural identity through their research (Schlosser, Lyons, Talleyrand, Kim, & Johnson, 2011a).

Clash of the Historians

After a rocky departure from the history department at a major research institution, Erica took her complementary MA degree and headed for other options. Entering another history program at another institution would likely produce the same unsettling outcome so she found what seemed to be a close fit in a school of education. She anticipated an opportunity for a more welcoming environment and the chance to apply her skills to historical foundations in their k–higher curriculum. Her goal of an academic position could still be realized. She anticipated meeting her assigned advisor, Professor Turner. Turns out, Turner held a doctorate in history which was why he agreed to take her on as an advisee. Erica's previous experience clouded her thinking but she decided after meeting with Turner that she would not make any hasty decisions. From her previous experience she knew it was unwise to switch advisors but with her lingering concerns she wondered if it would affect this relationship and prevent her from realizing her goal. Ironically, Professor Turner had a similar distaste for the history department based upon his own experiences. So they each had more in common than they realized but initially neither shared their concerns with one another.

McAlpine and Norton (2006) noted the powerful significance of the faculty/student relationship which is mitigated through the professional field or disciplinary area and the departmental culture. However, the collective academic department culture may not meet student needs or expectations, as was Erica's case with the history department. Furthermore, individual faculty and the department may assume that students know what they are getting themselves into when they matriculate to a graduate program, which may be a shortsighted and erroneous assumption on the part of faculty and administration that serves to hinder the development of a strong faculty/student relationship.

Interpersonal aspects of the faculty/student relationship should first include some foundation or similarity that each person shares in common. Pairing Erica with Professor Turner seemed appropriate. Support from the faculty member as well as opportunities for the advisor to challenge the advisee should be evident (Golde, 1994). While this would likely happen, neither Turner nor Erica took the first step in clearing the air and sharing their personal story. The potential to switch advisors looms in this case without a frank discussion.

Each student needs varying amounts of attention from faculty, some requiring less and others requiring more. In this case, Turner assumed Erica needed less than she might have required or desired, at least initially. More importantly, how faculty perceives their role takes precedent in the relationship. Tenenbaum, Crosby, and Gliner (2001) explored how faculty helped students network in their field, what social and psychological support faculty offered, and what job-related assistance faculty provided students. The faculty/student relationship should engender opportunities for the faculty to prepare the student for the intended professional role but admitted students need to function within the program first (Schlosser et al, 2011a; Weidman, Twale, & Stein, 2001). Initially, Erica needed the psycho-social support from Turner which Tenenbaum et al found comes more from female than male faculty. Length of time in graduate school also affected student satisfaction with faculty but unless a bond forms early in the relationship, dissatisfaction, disengagement, and departure often follow.

MITIGATING SOCIAL DISTANCE IN THE FACULTY/STUDENT RELATIONSHIP

Faculty/student relationships may be more difficult to form depending upon perceived or established affective closeness more so than physical closeness of the faculty and student. Social distance refers to a professional relationship with concomitant interaction at the median point between two parties (Bogardus, 1947). The *perception* of social distance between the faculty and student can be framed by the presence of either intergroup harmony or intergroup conflict. Furthermore, social distance can be experienced differently by cross-gender and cross-racial pairings (Golde, 1994, 1998, 2005). Social distance with faculty may be further shaped depending upon whether the student has a teaching or research assistantship or if the program is face to face or online.

While on campus relationships may be more easily developed, faculty's ability to establish and sustain relationships with students in distance learning formats may be as critical as it is challenging, especially when considering those same gender, race, status, and disciplinary differences. For instance, full-time students working in the department or highly visible in a department tend to establish a shorter social distance with faculty than part-time students, thus affecting the faculty/student relationship. This dynamic grows more complicated as students in online formats rarely see the faculty in person but must form and sustain strong, productive relationships anyway from a distance. Some departments hold more social gatherings for faculty and their graduate students to shrink social distance. Online formats cannot boast that luxury. Some programs instead encourage more professional interaction and collaboration on scholarly projects which can be more easily facilitated online. Socio-emotional distance between faculty and graduate students may be mitigated by disciplinary or professional area because some areas tend to be more warm and fuzzy than others (Slawski, 1973; Weidman et al, 2001).

In addition, faculty may be unaware that their personal disposition and demeanor in the classroom or the office sends subtle messages that can affect their relationship with students. Graduate students' *perceptions* of faculty actions can vary from the faculty's *intent* behind those actions. So student or faculty responses may be less than intended or inappropriate altogether. For instance, students may be expecting more cooperation and collaboration from faculty and express shock and dismay at the isolation and silos common to graduate faculty in prolific research departments. Faculty tending toward isolation may also send and display messages about the profession and academe that tend not to be what students expected when they entered the early stages of their program. These misread actions on the part of students and faculty may ultimately cast aspersions on the faculty/student relationship (Perna & Hudgins, 1996).

GENDER AND RACE AS FACTORS IN SOCIAL DISTANCE

Graduate students and faculty should recognize the boundaries of their relationships in order to separate appropriate behaviors (professional, academic, social, counseling, advising, supervising, business) from inappropriate interactions (exploitative, harassing, dating, intimate). Unfortunately, some of these behaviors/interactions still cause ambiguity, misinterpretation, and sensitivity along gender lines especially in cross-gender pairings (Holmes, Rupert, Ross, & Shapera, 1999).

Maher, Ford, and Thompson (2004) compared women who finished their PhD program on time with those who took considerably longer. Each group acknowledged supportive relationships as facilitating but also said the lack of a good faculty/student relationship constrained or hindered their progress. While appreciative of their experiences, women wished for greater richness and depth in their faculty/student relationships (Hagedorn, 1999). In another study, men reported being more satisfied with their faculty/student relationships but they sought out more time with faculty than did the women (Benkin, Beazley, & Jordan, 2000).

Ellis (2001) determined that race affects interactions with faculty and peers. Insufficient faculty relationships in the student's department forced some students to look outside their department to form relationships. In general, a poor sense of community in the department hindered the relationship for women and women of color more so than found among majority and minority males. White males expressed greater satisfaction with their advisor than did the other groups studied. Connections seemed difficult to facilitate and sustain and often minority females in particular reported feelings of isolation and greater social distance.

33

Diversity within the student body affects the faculty/student relationship. To employ a one-size-fits-all model for all students should be avoided or the relationship will be confusing and strained for both parties. As such, faculty should place greater importance on the student's cultural and social identity and the need to preserve it within their relationship (Schlosser et al, 2011a).

BRIDGING SOCIAL DISTANCE IN THE FACULTY/STUDENT RELATIONSHIP

Schlosser and Kahn (2007) noted that student research mastery and interest in researching helped create a stronger faculty/student alliance. Taking a different stance, Rhoades (2008) indicated that faculty entrepreneurialism in research, especially in the sciences, alters the faculty/student relationship. Specifically, when faculty researchers cultivate a commercial interest in their work rather than perform it purely for scholarly advancement, the use of graduate students in the process of that research entails a more business/management/labor stance rather than an academic supervisor/apprentice connection. Challenges to the old boundaries of supervisor/apprentice emerge and can muddy the relationship if the graduate student becomes an employee. Therefore, faculty/student relationship boundaries need to be adjusted or reestablished for maximum benefit. On the flip side, the sphere of influence of these faculty researchers may be passed to their graduate students thus enhancing their apprenticeship status.

Students reported greater verbal and non-verbal immediacy and less psychosocial distance with female faculty, which ultimately promoted a related sense of closeness between students and faculty (Jaasma & Koper, 2002). Jaasma and Koper posited that female faculty may see the faculty/student relationship as more equal and less hierarchical than male advisors. Faculty perceived to have greater immediacy tended to draw students to them, helping to create a tighter bond.

TWIG (1996) suggested the student/faculty relationship be less hierarchical and evaluative and more collaborative in nature. Increasing the type and variety of interaction between student and faculty enriches the relationship. Thinking of the faculty/student relationship as a process or journey is one way to form a stronger faculty/student bond. Forming this bond entails greater sharing of one's professional and personal self, seeking a comfort level, and minimizing the power differential between faculty and student.

MONITORING THE FACULTY/STUDENT RELATIONSHIP

Goldhamer and Shils (1939) referred to the differential in the faculty/student relationships as domination (as opposed to force or manipulation), meaning that faculty has *influence* over students. Bierstedt (1940) offered a clearer delineation that separates Goldhamer and Shils' influence from *power*. Power entails sociological significance whereas influence entails a psychological significance. Power comes from group controls whereas influence is exercised from personal faculty control. Status in the academic organization defines one's power but in one's role, influence can be played out through faculty temperament. Both faculty and student recognize the legitimacy of the unilateral power between them and the consequences of non-compliance, thus motivating conformity to behavioral norms and expectations (Bierstedt, 1940).

Warren (2005) also noted the unidirectional nature of the faculty/student relationship. Faculty exercises power over students who, new to the academic routine, may acquiesce to faculty influence. However, Baxter-Magolda (1996) noted the mutual respect found in the faculty/student relationship transcends the power differential.

Rosen and Bates (1967) considered the nature of the academic organization as the prime socializer of new entrants which greatly affects the relationship between faculty and students. They indicated that the faculty/student relationship functions on principles of "division of labor, the expression of affect, flow of communication, the nature and distribution of power and authority, and the degree of consensus and conflict" (Rosen & Bates, 1967, p. 72). These principles are necessary if the student is to acquire the knowledge and skills from the faculty to perform eventually in the professional role (Weidman et al, 2001). *How* they are delivered speaks to the faculty/student relationship.

Students learn from faculty with whom they come in contact, that is, professors, advisors, supervisors, chairs (Austin, 2002). Entering graduate students, already steeped in their studies, rarely see the complete picture of academic life from the faculty perspective or grasp how the departmental culture shapes their program. Faculty shows students what they need to see with regard to research and the professional field/standards of practice but other significant cultural details may often be veiled.

Rupert and Holmes (1997) wondered how institutions and professional associations structure those relationships. Clearly, professional faculty/student relationships need to remain professional in both advising and supervision. In the absence of guidelines, ambiguity and gray areas surface with little attention to the risks faced by students, advisors, the graduate school, or the institution.

In the presence of the power differential, faculty/student relationships can potentially cross acceptable boundaries. Faculty and students may experience confusion as to where professional boundaries begin and end. This does not suggest that the long-standing tradition of faculty autonomy and authority should be diminished or eliminated but rather, at the very least, it must be monitored (Cahn, 1994; Chiang, 2009; Whitley & Oddi, 1998). Cahn indicated that since faculty reviews each other's credentials for academic purposes, they should be willing and poised to evaluate and review colleagues' actions toward graduate students.

Monitoring faculty/student relationships should also exist as part of the widely accepted academic peer review process. In defense of faculty, their actions may have noble intentions as they believe their position affords them such luxury. However, inappropriate behaviors resulting from boundary crossing in the faculty/student relationship should not be tolerated, overlooked, or excused. However, colleagues often choose not to police those boundaries with another colleague, failing to see anything wrong. Thus, they decline to acknowledge the situation.

Inherent in a faculty/student relationship, the student possesses the freedom to stay or leave. Strauss (1964) recognized "that the student has the final responsibility of judging when the coaching relationship is genuinely harmful to himself or to his 'potential'" (p. 414). However, risk may be incurred or some price paid to secure that freedom even though staying may result in angst and uncertainty. The thought of termination and the actual severing of the faculty/student relationship may cause consternation as well as repercussions for the student more so than the faculty (Wolff, 1950). Any dissent or deviation from normative expectations might risk self-imposed alienation and perhaps alienation from faculty, administration, and peers (Lovitts, 2001).

Star Professor and the Unsuspecting

Professor Proudhomme, a self-proclaimed, self-aggrandized, highly published professor, occasionally accepted student advisees only in his specialized area of scholarship. His consulting schedule, speaking engagements, and research productivity rendered his free time minimal, which meant that meetings with doctoral students outside of class had to be scheduled well in advance, and often were cancelled and rescheduled. Meetings lasted no more than 30 minutes with several interruptions for him to accept in-coming phone calls from foreign dignitaries and other very important people. Students eager to work under Proudhomme's tutelage never anticipated that the brief but sterile environment he offered would affect their ability to formulate a dissertation proposal, receive guidance from him once the proposal was accepted, or cultivate a strong collegial bond.

In the Allen and Smith (2008) study, students wanted faculty to know them as individuals. Students expected faculty to care about their well-being; however, faculty with large advising loads had difficulty doing so. Professor Proudhomme's reputation entices students but it may not guarantee the strong faculty/student bond the student needs, desires, or deserves. In fact, it may signal the opposite, that is, dissatisfaction, disengagement, or departure. Rice et al (2009) reported that students desired greater rather than minimal faculty accessibility, feedback, and guidance. Students aligned positively with faculty when they helped them get financial support as well as provided them with academic and emotional support and assisted with cultural adjustment.

Brackman, Nunez, and Basu (2010) found graduate students also desired spending more time with their faculty advisor, but students realized that advisor time came at a premium. Unfortunately, less time with an advisor like Proudhomme ultimately hinders student progress to the degree. Students also recognized the potential for conflict in their relationship with faculty so many avoided discussing certain topics, acquiesced to their advisor's suggestions, and sought alternative forms of support through their peers and others. As is typical, faculty seldom has the same kind of relationship with all of their students. At least Proudhomme was selective in the students he did accept; however, his focus allowed little opportunity for them to bond effectively.

A Relationship Gone Sour

Being on the management department's admission committee proved to be more of a blessing than a chore for Professor Vrabel. It provided her with opportunity not only to assemble each fall's entering doctoral cohort but also to connect with them during the interview process. One admitted student, Fran, requested Vrabel as his advisor. Fran held a high-profile job outside the field of higher education in a predominantly male-dominated profession. Through coursework, plan of study meetings, and comp preparation, Fran treated Vrabel with respect that seemed fine initially but later appeared to Vrabel to be more condescending than respectful. Despite her growing concerns, she tried to remain objective about the situation and their association. Fran's business donated items to her charity event one spring which she accepted but wondered why he made the gesture. She wondered if he had an ulterior motive. When Fran failed to pass the comprehensive examination, he blamed Vrabel and sought a male advisor who would surely have *his* best interests at heart.

Damrosch (1995) described the faculty/student relationship as an old tradition of mentor to disciple, that is, "a mutually illuminating and informing relationship *when it works*" (p. 173, emphasis added). Nesheim (2006), however, noted the "essential but volatile nature of relationships with faculty" (p. 11). Ahmad (2007) recognized that faculty/student relationships can become strained and broken. Perhaps Fran and Professor Vrabel crossed the line of propriety with the giving and receiving of "gifts" even though they were designated for charity. As a result, the student may respond with obstinacy and ignore faculty direction or sever communication. While these behaviors show disrespect and professional immaturity, they remain commonplace responses. However, faculty must counsel these students whether the student remains or departs. Only Fran knows the motivation behind his actions but Vrabel should have checked policy to see if receiving Fran's seemingly harmless "gifts" could be construed as inappropriate. This altered their faculty/student relationship in ways that necessitated administrative intervention and the reformation of the dyad midway through Fran's program which raised the potential for a negative outcome.

In summary, the faculty/student relationship should promote student self-efficacy and autonomy through coursework and assistantships, inculcate competence in the research area and professional practice, and offer opportunities for presenting and publishing. Beyond these basics, faculty should be interested in graduating leaders in the field, good professional citizens, and promotable practitioners. These, in turn, enhance the program, department, profession, and faculty reputation (Schlosser et al, 2011a).

BEST PRACTICES

- Strong faculty/student relationships take time and effort. Administratively, faculty time for advising, supervising, and chairing needs should be factored into faculty workload (Richardson, MacRae, Schwartz, Bankston, & Kosten, 2008).
- Understanding the faculty/student relationship needs to be researched further. Davidson and Foster-Johnson (2001) suggested program benchmarking, evaluating, and updating as part of that research. Influences of increased diversity, accountability, and technology in the academic workplace that will affect the faculty/student relationship should also be researched further (Austin & McDaniels, 2006).
- Davidson and Foster-Johnson (2001) recommended that faculty/student cross-gender and cross-race relationships necessitate faculty attendance at diversity seminars in order to address social, emotional, and psychological distance.
- Faculty and administration must devise ground rules that address the nature of the power/influence differential in the faculty/student relationship (TWIG, 1996). Without a clear policy statement above and beyond the implied ethical code of conduct for many professions and academics, little can be clearly identified or remedied (Cahn, 1994).
- To address faculty/student relationships as a retention concern, a student assessment of the relationship and/or an exit interview with administration following the student's point of departure would be illuminating (Sutton & Sankar, 2011).

RESOURCES

- For information on an instrument that assesses faculty/student relationships in terms of student satisfaction with their faculty advisor and supervisor, see Tenenbaum et al (2001).
- To view a Bogardus Social Distance Scale, visit www.socialdistancesurvey.com/ (retrieved November 24, 2014).
- Check your campus faculty handbook for more information on policies involving the faculty/student relationship boundaries.

38

REFERENCES

Ahmad, K. (2007). *PhD: The pursuit of excellence*. Singapore: Thompson Learning Asia.

Allen, J., & Smith, C. (2008). Faculty and student perspectives on advising: Implications for student dissatisfaction. *Journal of College Student Development, 49*, 609–624.

Austin, A. (2002). Preparing the next generation of faculty: Graduate school as socialization to the academic career. *Journal of Higher Education, 73*, 94–122.

Austin, A., & McDaniels, M. (2006). Preparing the professoriat of the future: Graduate student socialization for faculty roles. In J. Smart (Ed.), *Higher education handbook of theory and research*, Volume 21 (pp. 397–456). Dordrecht, Netherlands: Springer.

Baxter-Magolda, M. (1996). Epistemological development in graduate and professional education. *Review of Higher Education, 19*, 283–304.

Benkin, E., Beazley, J., & Jordan, P. (2000, February). Doctoral students rate their dissertation chairs: Analysis by gender. In *Graduate Focus: Issues in Graduate Education*. Los Angeles: UCLA Graduate Division. (ERIC Document Reproduction Service No. ED464 576)

Bierstedt, R. (1940). Analysis of power. *American Sociological Review, 15,* 730–738.

Bogardus, E. (1947). Measurement of personal-group relations. *Sociometry, 10,* 306–311.

Brackman, J., Nunez, A., & Basu, A. (2010). Effectiveness of a conflict resolution training program in changing graduate student style of managing conflict with faculty advisors. *Innovative Higher Education, 35*, 277–293.

Cahn, S. (1994). *Saints and scamps*. Lanham, MD: Rowman & Littlefield.

Chiang, S. (2009). Personal power and positional power in a power-full "I": A discourse analysis of doctoral dissertation supervision. *Discourse and Communication, 3,* 255–272.

Damrosch, D. (1995). *We scholars: Changing the culture of the university*. Cambridge, MA: Harvard University Press.

Davidson, M., & Foster-Johnson, L. (2001). Mentoring in the preparation of graduate researchers of color. *Review of Educational Research, 71*, 549–574.

Descutnes, C., & Thelen, M. (1989). Graduate student and faculty perspectives about graduate school. *Teaching of Psychology, 16*(2), 58–61.

Ellis, E. (2001). The impact of race and gender on graduate school socialization, satisfaction with doctoral study, and commitment to degree completion. *The Western Journal of Black Studies, 25*, 30–45.

Galbraith, M. W. (2003). The adult education professor as mentor: A means to enhance teaching and learning. *Perspectives: The New York Journal of Adult Learning, 1*(1), 9–20.

Golde, C. (1994, November). *Student description of the doctoral student attrition process*. Paper presented at the annual meeting of the Association for the Study of Higher Education, Tucson. (ERIC Document Reproduction Service No. ED375 733)

Golde, C. (1998). Beginning graduate school: Explaining first year doctoral attrition. In M. Anderson (Ed.), *The experience of being in graduate school: An exploration* (pp. 55–64). New Directions for Higher Education no. 101. Amherst, NY: Prometheus Books.

Golde, C., (2005). The role of the department and discipline in doctoral student attrition: Lessons from four departments. *Journal of Higher Education, 76,* 669–701.

Goldhamer, H., & Shils, E. (1939). Types of power and status. *American Journal of Sociology, 45,* 171–182.

Hagedorn, L.S. (1999). Factors related to the retention of female graduate students over 30. *Journal of College Student Retention, 1,* 99–44.

Heathcott, J. (2007). Blueprints, tools, and the reality before us: Improving doctoral education in the humanities. *Change, 39*(5), 46–51.

Holmes, D., Rupert, P., Ross, S., & Shapera, W. (1999). Student perceptions of dual relationships between faculty and students. *Ethics and Behavior, 9,* 79–107.

Jaasma, M., & Koper, R. (2002). Out-of-class communication between female and male students and faculty: The relationship to student perceptions of instructional immediacy. *Women's Studies in Communication, 25,* 119–137.

Lovitts, B. (2001). *Leaving the ivory tower: The causes and consequences of departure from doctoral study.* Lanham, MD: Rowman-Littlefield.

Maher, M., Ford, M., & Thompson, C. (2004). Degree progress of women doctoral students: Factors that constrain, facilitate, and differentiate. *Review of Higher Education, 27,* 385–408.

McAlpine, L., & Norton, J. (2006). Reframing our approach to doctoral programs: An integrative framework for action and research. *Higher Education Research and Development, 25*(1), 3–17.

Nesheim, B. (2006). If you want to know. In M. Guentzel & B. Neisham (Eds.), *Supporting graduate and professional students: The role of student affairs* (pp. 5–19). New Direction for Student Services no. 115. Hoboken, NJ: Wiley & Sons.

Nettles, M., & Millett, C. (2006). *Three magic letters: Getting the Ph.D.* Baltimore: Johns Hopkins University Press.

Perna, L., & Hudgins, C. (1996, November). *The graduate assistantship: Facilitator of graduate students' professional socialization.* Paper presented at the annual meeting of the Association for the Study of Higher Education, Memphis, TN. (ERIC Document Reproduction Service No. ED402 822)

Rhoades, G. (2008). The study of the academic profession. In P. Gumport (Ed.), *Sociology of higher education* (pp. 113–146). Baltimore: Johns Hopkins University Press.

Rice, K., Choi, C., Zhang, Y., Villegas, J., Huen, J., Anderson, D., Nesic, A., & Bigler, M. (2009). International student perspectives on graduate advising relationships. *Journal of Counseling Psychology, 56,* 376–391.

Richardson, P., MacRae, A., Schwartz, K., Bankston, L., & Kosten, C. (2008). Student outcomes in a post-professional online master's-degree program. *The American Journal of Occupational Therapy, 62,* 600–610.

Rosen, B., & Bates, A. (1967). The structure of socialization in graduate school. *Social Inquiry, 37*, 71–84.

Rupert, P., & Holmes, D. (1997). Dual relationships in higher education: Professional and institutional guidelines. *Journal of Higher Education, 68*, 660–678.

Schlosser, L., & Kahn, J. (2007). Dyadic perspectives in advisor–advisee relationships in counseling psychology doctoral programs. *Journal of Counseling Psychology, 54*, 211–217.

Schlosser, L., Lyons, H., Talleyrand, R., Kim, B., & Johnson, W.B. (2011a). A multicultural infused model of graduate advising relationships. *Journal of Career Development, 38*, 44–61.

Schlosser, L., Lyons, H., Talleyrand, R., Kim, B., & Johnson, W.B. (2011b). Advisor–advisee relationships in graduate training programs. *Journal of Career Development, 38*, 3–18.

Slawski, C. (1973, August). *Personal socialization in organizational context: Hypotheses and comparative cases.* Paper presented at the annual meeting of the American Psychological Association, New York. (ERIC Document Reproduction Service No. ED157 451)

Strauss, A. (1964). Regularized status-passage. In W. Bennis, E. Schein, D. Berlow, & F. Steele (Eds.), *Interpersonal dynamics* (pp. 409–416). Homewood, IL: Dorsey Press.

Sutton, K., & Sankar, C. (2011). Student satisfaction with information provided by academic advisors. *Journal of STEM Education, 12*(7/8), 71–86.

Tenenbaum, H., Crosby, F., & Gliner, M. (2001). Mentoring relationships in graduate school. *Journal of Vocational Behavior, 59*, 326–341.

TWIG Writing Group. (1996). A feminist perspective on graduate student–advisor relationships. *Feminist Teacher, 10*, 17–25.

Warren, E.S. (2005). Future colleague or convenient friend: The ethics of mentorship. *Counseling and Values, 49*, 141–146.

Weidman, J., Twale, D., & Stein, E. (2001). *Socialization of graduate and professional students in higher education: A perilous passage?* San Francisco: Jossey-Bass.

Whitley, G., & Oddi, L (1998). Graduate student–faculty collaboration in research and publication. *Western Journal of Nursing, 20*, 572–583.

Wolff, K. (1950). *The sociology of Georg Simmel.* Glencoe, IL: The Free Press.

41

Chapter 4

Working Together

Faculty Advisor and Graduate Advisee

Prior to the formal graduate school at the university, research institutes recruited students as apprentices under the tutelage of professors who oversaw seminars or laboratories depending upon their discipline (Parsons & Platt, 1973). Increases in doctoral degrees during the first half of the 20th century necessitated more standard curriculums and requirements in order to uphold the value of the degree. Doctors of Philosophy reserved for academic placement eventually spawned the practitioner degree, for example, the Doctor of Education, the Psychology Doctorate, and the slower to achieve recognition, Doctor of Arts (Brubaker & Rudy, 1997). Graduate education proliferated through additional professional areas which flourished off the pre-professional majors in medicine, law, dentistry, religion, veterinary medicine, pharmacy, and occupational and physical therapy (Geiger, 2007).

Academic degree programs share something in common, however: It takes less time and psychic energy to advise master's students than it does doctoral students (O'Meara, Knudsen, & Jones, 2013) because course advising differs from thesis/dissertation advising (Richardson, MacRae, Schwartz, Bankston, & Kosten, 2008). Advising doctoral students adds extra burdens to faculty schedules because more attention is given to admitting students, matching faculty and student research interests, formulating plans of study, reaching candidacy, overseeing research, professionalizing students, and perhaps collaborating, presenting, and publishing with them.

In addition, original research separates doctoral scholars from master's degree holders. Therefore, master's students may have shorter, more prescribed programs with varying exit expectations ranging from written and/or oral comprehensive exams, a research project, or a thesis that requires differing levels of faculty time (Jackson & Scheel, 2013). Advising master's students, however, serves as the ideal time to recognize doctoral potential and begin to encourage students to consider further study.

Some master's programs serve as cash cows. In order to pay for some doctoral programs, master's programs have expanded to meet student consumer demands and increase departmental budgets. However, that does not mean that the master's student should be overlooked in order to reserve time and energy for the doctoral student. Advising doctoral students requires different types of skills than would normally be expended in master's programs.

The advisor/advisee alliance to accomplish program goals changes with each stage. Advising to schedule coursework and sign the approved plan of study entails less skill or emotional investment than working with students collaboratively to complete a grant-funded project, a thesis/dissertation proposal, a successful defense, or a conference paper. In fact, *how* the advisor and advisee relate during the basic advising stages following matriculation offers implications for *how well* the student will internalize the research or professional emphasis of their program reserved for the latter stages of their journey (Schlosser & Kahn, 2007). These circumstances set the stage for the advisor/advisee relationship.

Too Long for Howard

The department held to a hard and fast rule: three years from course completion to the formal dissertation proposal committee meeting. Student and graduate assistant for longer than anyone could remember, Howard dreaded meeting with his advisor or passing committee members in the corridor. They always asked when they could expect a draft of his proposal. He didn't have any clue how to go about narrowing his idea to a manageable topic. One week prior to that three-year deadline, he initiated a conversation with one of his GA supervisors, Professor Long. She was relatively new so she had no idea about Howard's history or his impending proposal deadline. Howard posed his research ideas to her hoping she could magically pull a great cutting-edge topic out of her briefcase. Long heard Howard's ideas and realized his years in the program had not served him well. She questioned why he was not having this conversation with his advisor and why he wasted the last three years. Howard replied that his advisor seemed critical and dismissive of his efforts and made him feel inadequate and incapable.

DEFINING THE ADVISOR/ADVISEE ROLE RELATIONSHIP

Graduate school advisors can either offer their students the keys to their future or unknowingly hinder their forward progress. Noy and Ray (2012) identify six categories of faculty advisors: (1) the affective therapist who is concerned with student well-being; (2) the instrumental advocate who promotes the master/apprentice model; (3) the intellectual researcher who guides and models the student inquiry process; (4) the available, timely communicator who keeps students in the loop; (5) the respectful supporter of all diverse student groups; and (6) the exploitative user who furthers his/her own agenda at the students' expense. While the first five categories offer something positive and valuable to the student, the sixth type should be avoided. Howard's advisor fell into this category. His advisor knew that Howard was not progressing and could have directed him to another advisor. Because Howard could not form a researchable dissertation topic, other faculty was reluctant to accept him. Policy permitted him to stay the full length the program allowed but the added time would never produce a positive outcome. Jenks and Riesman (1977) reasoned that "some doctoral candidates are kept around too long out of compassion or favoritism or indifference to their fate" (p. 537). Also, Howard placed Long, an untenured faculty member, in a precarious position. She was wise to decline direction in the interest of her own departmental position.

Brown and Krager (1985) detailed the faculty role as advisor, instructor, curriculum planner, researcher, and mentor. Faculty fulfills these aspects of this multifaceted role when they interface with students. In performance of these role stipulations, faculty can exercise autonomy or "cause harm through action and inaction" on behalf of the students they advise, as did Howard's faculty advisor (p. 406). The faculty role presupposes the need to treat students equally and offer them support through the critical phases of their program, especially through dissertation defense. To be fair, the student must reciprocate. Howard's advisor could have interpreted Howard's behavior as not fulfilling his obligations to progress through the program and thus stopped helping Howard. Similarly, Howard felt little guidance in return so he exhausted the time until his absolute deadline. His situation highlights the reciprocity and communication needed to make the advisor/advisee relationship successful.

Advisors agreed that preparation for their advising role emerged from previous experience and exposure to advising styles rather than to formal training (Knox, Schlosser, Pruitt, & Hill, 2006; O'Meara et al, 2013). Unfortunately, advisors remain unprepared for the procedural as well as for the emotional component associated with advising. On the flip side, students rarely receive any training as to how to relate and interact with their faculty advisor (O'Meara et al, 2013) as Howard's situation illustrates.

No Two are Alike

Liz and Carl worked for the same firm and decided to go back together for their masters. Even though they enrolled in the same program, Liz's advisor was Professor Pavuk and Professor Batson advised Carl. Issues arose when Liz and Carl compared notes, only to realize they received different guidance on course requirements in the program. Carl noted that his advising sessions were more informal and longer than Liz's. Pavuk always seemed busy with his research to have much time for Liz. Batson often sent Carl email reminders and appeared genuinely interested in Carl's progress. Liz never received communication from Pavuk, so she talked to peers and learned that she was not alone. Instead of asking formally for a new advisor, Liz just went to Carl for advice and duplicated his schedule.

Wrench and Punyanunt (2004) noted that "graduate advisors help their advisees learn about the academic field, the university setting, research, ethics, and many other important aspects related to being an academic professional" (p. 225). Their study illustrated the life-changing, career-planning impact of a graduate faculty advisor. The authors stressed the need for mutual trust and honesty, and the perception of caring about the student's welfare, as well as helping the student make progress to successful outcomes. Batson cared about her students while Pavuk chose to divert his efforts to his research. Not formally choosing a new advisor, Liz depicts a department where switching advisors might prove risky to her future in the program. Perhaps Pavuk would be offended.

Damrosch (1995) argued that graduate education and, in this case, advising can seem cloudy and mystical. The graduate student is paired with a singular advisor with whom a productive relationship may or may not develop. A good relationship resulted in Carl's case but not Liz's and obviously other students in her program. Being a poor advisor may not preclude Pavuk from doing the rest of his job very well, but it may preclude Liz from completing her program on time or at all. Although Pavuk may be a superior researcher, as Liz's assigned advisor he also needs to provide Liz with accurate information and support.

Just Trying to be Helpful

Sometimes Professor Smetana found it difficult to be an advisor *and* an evaluator of that same student's work. How she related to students in her office indicated to her how she wanted to be regarded, that is, helpful, knowledgeable about program specifics and university policy, and understanding. When she handed back papers to students who performed poorly in class, she realized that it could and often did affect her advising relationship with them. She believed her feedback on assignments should be specific in order to help students improve their work but comments critiquing that work may not be received well. Vilma performed well in online class discussion formats but her written assignments needed work. Smetana counseled Vilma to visit the campus writing center. Insulted, Vilma walked into Smetana's office unannounced and informed her that a friend of hers read her papers and declared them to be just fine. Vilma indicated she would be seeking another advisor.

Bennett (1998) acknowledged the professor can be caught in adversarial roles—teacher, advisor/mentor, and evaluator as Professor Smetana illustrates. Those who sit under a professor's tutelage are constantly evaluated, guided, evaluated, guided, and evaluated again. Mitigating the student qua student and student qua advisee may proceed smoothly or it may not, depending upon how well students fulfill *their* role and meet the professors' standard as student *and* advisee. Often the disparity comes when the student fails to realize the boundaries and expectations of the faculty role, that is, Smetana's obligation to Vilma in both roles. By the same token, Vilma acted irrationally and unprofessionally. Complications with the faculty/student connection never allowed the advisor/advisee relationship to develop further.

SUSTAINING THE ADVISOR/ADVISEE DYAD

Using Georg Simmel's seminal work on group interaction, Wolff (1950) interpreted the dyad, or two-person association, as a fragile entity. Because the dyad cannot exist without both parties, each party feels some obligation to do whatever needs to be done to sustain it. Some dyads exist with each party on an equal footing while other dyads necessitate a unidirectional power structure. Usually the superordinate, acquiring some measure of authority over the subordinate, garners trust and respect from the subordinate as a result of some appreciated special quality or expertise that the superordinate possesses that the subordinate desires to have. The advisor/advisee relationship formed in graduate school provides a good example of this unidirectional dyad.

The political and social realm in academe clearly distinguishes superordinate from subordinate. Status distinctions and formal relationships between faculty and graduate student abound within the department, the program, the lab, and the classroom (Murdock, 1960). Faculty power and influence often control graduate student destiny throughout the student's program.

The advisor/advisee connection encompasses multiple interactions that are serialized: Previous encounters between the dyad connect to current and future encounters focused around some situation or purpose (TWIG, 1996). This stratification implies differential treatment pending the advisee's inculcation and demonstration of prevailing academic norms. Students may experience difficulty switching from the early submission phase of the advisor/advisee relationship to the independent scholar phase without varying degrees of assistance from the faculty advisor. Strauss (1964) noted that paternalistic faculty tends to prolong stratification and neglectful faculty fails to oversee that inculcation process. As such, the student as professional may be degreed but clinically ill-equipped to perform adequately professionally. These situations reflect poorly on the advisor/supervisor and the department (Parsons & Platt, 1973).

STUDENTS AND FACULTY DESCRIBE GOOD ADVISING

Formally, good advisors should possess accountability, authenticity, and moral integrity (Harrison, 2012). Informally, good advisors should possess enough objective savvy and sensitivity to be able to assess if each advisee is receiving and also internalizing the basic aspects of the program and the discipline/field in order to determine how or if the advisor/advisee relationship should proceed (Schlosser & Kahn, 2007). Barrick, Clark, and Blaschek (2006) noted that students' ideal advisor provided more feedback and assistance and offered more emotional support. Advisors should be perceived by students as available by what, why, how, and how often they communicate with students. Rice et al (2009) reported overall student satisfaction with the advisor; however, some students wished the interpersonal dynamics could be improved.

Faculty advisors function ideally in three basic areas: (1) as an interpersonal communicator; (2) as a master to apprentice; and (3) as a stimulator of progress through tasks and rites of passage (Schlosser, Lyons, Talleyrand, Kim, & Johnson, 2011b). How well the advisor facilitates these areas can be assessed by the degree of smoothness and seamlessness he/she demonstrates in his/her purveyance. Connection between advisor and advisee must be mutual enough to facilitate a working relationship free from conflict (Schlosser, Lyons, Talleyrand, Kim, & Johnson, 2011a). For instance, the presence of trust and respect and little, if any, conflict signal a more positive advisor/advisee relationship. However, conflict in the relationship may not be detrimental depending upon how each party overcomes the conflict (Knox et al, 2006).

Good advising should open doors to student professionalization opportunities (Ellis, 2001). The advisor should guide the student toward self-efficacy and become a creator of new knowledge that further advances the field/discipline under their watchful guidance and expertise (Egan, 1989).

BENEFITS AND COSTS OF ADVISING

The presence or the absence of good advising by faculty can have concomitant positive or negative effects on graduate students (Faison, 1996; Ferreira, 2000; Luebs, Fredrickson, Hyon, & Samraj, 1998). But advising *is* a two-way street. For the advisor, the benefits to advising should outweigh the costs and ultimately produce satisfaction within the faculty member as a result of shepherding new scholars and practitioners (Schlosser et al, 2011b). Advising benefits for faculty include grateful advisees, personal satisfaction, and certain job-related incentives, such as research collaboration, co-authorship on cutting-edge research, and passing on the discipline to new generations of students (Knox et al, 2006).

However, advising graduate students comes with costs. For instance, advising is a time-consuming process that can drain faculty of physical and emotional energy and subtract time from one's own research interests, teaching preparation, and campus/professional service. These are critical concerns, especially in the absence of formal incentives or rewards (Knox et al, 2006). Advising requires the continued development of new and/or existing skill sets. If one's field of knowledge is to be advanced, faculty needs to advise in ways that encourage students to take risks and break new ground (Brackman, Nunez, & Basu, 2010).

A Tale of Two Students

Two part-time master's students, Leah and Abby, commuted to class together. With identical schedules, they took the same classes and had the same advisor, Professor Geyer. Class discussion and performance on assignments, however, differed. In addition, Abby experienced several physical, medical, and emotional setbacks during the program so Leah graduated first. In fact, Abby stopped out for over a year. Both expressed an interest in entering the doctoral program Geyer coordinated. He realized that Abby would have difficulty meeting the minimum requirements for admission based on her academic performance in the master's program. He was not sure how her personal situation would affect her continuance in a demanding doctoral program. In addition, while Leah could handle doctoral-level coursework, Geyer surmised that both of them would have no trouble getting admitted or handling the work because they would rely on each other. Because their undergraduate and master's degrees both came from this university, Geyer recommended they attend a different program. Furthermore, neither student really needed a doctorate to advance in their positions.

ADVISING DIVERSE AND CROSS-GENDER GROUPINGS

Faculty no longer has the luxury of advising homogeneous populations of students. Increases in a diverse applicant pool coupled with a pool of advisors who often lack the multicultural dynamics to relate well to students challenges the advisor/advisee relationship. As a result, faculty must adjust their advising efforts to reach a diversity of students. Age, race, gender, ethnicity, sexual orientation, religion, and citizenship render the advising role more challenging. Advising can be further complicated by full- versus part-time student status as well as meeting face to face or reaching students only online.

How much productive contact faculty has with students and how faculty encourage their advisees to progress depends on the expertise of the advisor, students' ability to utilize faculty advice wisely, and their collective interaction as an advisor/advisee team. Involvement may be sterile and minimal or quite varied and extensive as Geyer enjoyed with Abby and Leah.

Advisors help students with courses/program selection but may not always be the thesis/dissertation chair. Some advisors go on to serve as both and others take over later as chair (Schlosser et al, 2011b). Faculty must focus on honing their advising skills to ensure they guide these students with specific needs successfully through their program. In cross-gender pairings, Geyer looked at the academic aspects of the relationship rather than what the degree journey meant to Abby and Leah as a team. He provided good basic advice from his perspective but may have neglected to consider other elements important to Abby and Leah.

Johnson-Bailey, Valentine, Cervero, and Bowles (2009) suggested that campus administrations provide faculty with information on diversity issues that affect the advising/supervising of cross-race and cross-gender pairings and how these students relate to faculty, how they obtain their information about aspects of graduate programs, and how they communicate with faculty and administration.

STUDENTS AND FACULTY DESCRIBE THE POOR ADVISOR

Bowen and Rudenstine (1992) anticipated faculty advising to fall somewhere between the paternalistic professor who too closely monitors student progress (Professors Geyer and Batson) and the distant, passive laissez-faire advisor who spends too little time guiding the student's progress (Professors Proudhomme and Pavuk). Laissez-faire advisors allow students to fashion their own approach to graduate study and often postpone key rites of passage such as comprehensive exams, proposals, or the final defense. Programs harbor too many Howards, who fall into the post-comprehensive, ABD abyss. Faculty who tends to be more authoritarian with students manages to either get students to finish their programs on time *or* successfully culls the department's/profession's herd of students.

Unpredictable describes some faculty advisors. Unfortunately, students have no idea in what mood they will find their advisor so they remain cautious about meeting with and/or sharing certain personal or professional information. Furthermore, ineffective advisors cause students like Liz to seek information elsewhere, information which could prove inaccurate or conflicting. While comfort levels increased over time for satisfied advisees, unsatisfied advisees grew more distant and cautious with their advisors causing students to long for accessibility and consistency (Schlosser, Knox, Moskowitz, & Hill, 2003).

Relationships function on the quality of interpersonal competence as well as the frequency with which advisor/advisee meetings occur as a means to accomplish program business (Schlosser et al, 2003). Faculty should be mindful of what their demeanor communicates to their advisees and vice versa in these meetings. For instance, faculty should not come across as aggressive, disinterested, preoccupied, overworked, confused, and/or dictatorial (Cassuto, 2012). On the flip side, faculty longed to avoid advisees who appeared "anxious, presumptuous, rigid, lazy, self-centered, irresponsible, avoidant, dependent, had poor work habits, and lacked clear boundaries" and displayed resistance, disrespect, conflict, poor preparation and communication, embarrassment, academic dishonesty, personality clashes, immaturity, unpreparedness for graduate-level work, poor work ethic, betrayal, misrepresentation, power struggles, and dysfunctional behavior (Knox et al, 2006, p. 504). Both faculty and students need to work on their interpersonal communication in order to avoid negative behaviors and instead strengthen the advisor/advisee relationship.

EFFECTS OF THE DEPARTMENT CLIMATE ON THE ADVISOR/ADVISEE RELATIONSHIP

Because graduate students function within a department rather than university wide as in the case of undergraduates, the policies set forth by graduate schools and department faculty regulate graduate study. Intellectual activity in neighboring departments differs as do expectations for professional or disciplinary credentialing. Differences exist as a result of basic requirements for the degree, assistantships offered, advising practices and good advisor matches, peer support, available mentoring, and academic culture and organizational climate (Ferrer de Valero, 2001; Hermanowicz, 2005). With these differences it is difficult to make assumptions or generalizations.

Boyle and Boice (1995) determined that departmental climate had an effect on subsequent student success in a program. Lovitts (2001) acknowledged that some departmental cultures are more welcoming and inclusive than others. Anderson and Swazey (1998) learned that organizational climates varied by program. For instance, chemistry students experienced a collaborative atmosphere compared to sociology graduate students who rarely experienced one. Sociology students described faculty as competitive and self-interested, forcing students to "compete for faculty time and attention" which subsequently they learned was not evenly distributed among them (p. 6). Ferrer de Valero (2001) discovered "that the department environment in the high-competition departments [engineering, chemistry, biology] was warm and supportive, whereas the environment in the low-competition departments [economics, physics, finance, psychology] was efficient and professional" (p. 316). Great departmental environments portend higher student satisfaction and program completion rates.

Faculty interprets the nature of faculty work, the pressure to publish, the workplace, work/life balance, and service differently than administration does rendering dissonance and a possible misinterpretation. How individual faculty deals with advising issues may diverge from how the organizational culture or departmental climate deals with them. This dissonance may lead to conflict for which faculty revert back to their personal response system when resolving it, placing the advisor and advisee in jeopardy (Tierney, 1997).

50

IMPROVING ADVISING THROUGH EVALUATION

Because good advising can be linked to graduate student success, tools to evaluate advising and determine quality advising should be constructed (Harrison, 2012). Differences between advising disciplines and professions may necessitate the creation of specific tools to capture subtle nuances in each field. Academic doctorates require an advisor overseeing an individual student. Professional doctorates focus more on team problem-solving approaches with one assigned faculty advisor and additional practitioners becoming involved later in the program. Given this non-traditional approach to advising, not only must faculty adapt to a new advising role but also graduate programs must provide clearly written guidelines for students, faculty, and practitioners as well as incorporate concomitant evaluation (Everson, 2009).

Existing instruments measure graduate advising in terms of faculty knowledge base; faculty availability, organization, and approachability; faculty nurturance; and effective faculty communication and advocacy. However, these may need to be augmented by discipline and department to include program-specific information. Measuring these qualities may be helpful to a faculty member. However, feelings and attitudes of their advisees, individually and/or collectively, over time also need to be measured (Schlosser & Kahn, 2007).

Marsh, Rowe, and Martin (2002) found that students evaluated their advisor similarly due to the individual nature of the relationship. So while the results of the evaluation might be helpful to one professor, aggregate sample data offer little information that would be helpful to all program faculty or the department. Reproducible results over time would likely never occur because comparing the collective of students an advisor advises proves difficult given how different each student is from another. However, advisors *have* the capacity to compare their past advising relationships with current relationships and make appropriate adaptations and adjustments based on those cumulative experiences. Instruments could be fashioned similar to those used in evaluations of teaching and used for personal and professional development purposes.

Faculty should evaluate their own track record as an advisor (Barres, 2013). Advisor self-evaluation can potentially aid in a more satisfying advisor/advisee relationship. Self-evaluation encompasses the initial advisor choice of advisees as well as subsequent choices needed as students move through the program (Schlosser et al, 2003; Schlosser et al, 2011a).

Faculty may excel at certain aspects of the role but not at others. This may serve as a guide when taking on new students or accepting transfers from colleagues. Faculty must take time to talk to their advisees and determine if the relationship is solid and progressing forward, or determine if the student needs reassignment, should stop out for a specified period of time, or should transfer to another program or university (Barres, 2013). Matching the student with the proper

51

advisor at any point in the student's program affects satisfaction, persistence, and the faculty/student relationship (Sutton & Sankar, 2011; Zhao, Golde, & McCormick, 2007).

BEST PRACTICES

- New scholars will have to incorporate more skills into their roles that include sustaining good advisor/advisee relationships. Therefore, this calls for preparation during graduate training or during the first years of teaching by pairing new faculty with seasoned faculty advisors and offering advising workshops (Austin & McDaniels, 2006).

- Matching advisors with advisees might be facilitated through regularly scheduled departmental forums and research days. This can provide an opportunity for faculty to acquaint students with their research interests and the rigors of independent scholarship (Crum & Franklin, 2002). Written information on faculty interests should be available and readily accessible to students. Attention to cross-race and cross-gender pairings should be considered.

- During the orientation meeting, advisors and their advisees should set goals that they need to achieve as a collective. Through evaluation over time, advisors and advisees can acknowledge unrealistically set goals (Austin & McDaniels, 2006) and revise accordingly.

- Sutton and Sankar (2011) suggested, where possible, that advisors ask students what they expect from the advising experience: a professional mentor, career advice, or faculty/student collaboration. Faculty advisors may need to focus on their own weak points to give students a more well-rounded skill set to take with them.

- Periodic evaluation of advising should be as consistent as evaluation of teaching and reviewed during annual performance appraisals.

- Faculty should consider advising students using more group/cohort seminars especially in prescribed master's programs. Advising may be expressed in group/team efforts and held less frequently throughout the program. Beginning formally at orientation, all students can receive the same information at the same time. Hard copy or web-accessible comprehensive handbooks should exist, be referenced, and periodically revised to assist master's students. Sessions should be attended by new as well as current students (Levin, 2008).

- Formalized administrative mechanisms should be highly visible in the department and include opportunities like seminars, social opportunities, and safety nets all designed to assist, support, and ensure more effective advisor/advisee relationships. Mechanisms to garner faculty involvement in more effective advising may be needed as well as include recognition and awards for meritorious service on student theses/dissertations (Tierney, 1997; Walker, Golde, Jones, Bueschel, & Hutchings, 2008).

RESOURCES

- To locate assessments for alumni, enrolled doctoral students, non-persisting students, and programs measuring satisfaction, critical thinking, choice processes, ethical behavior, and social development, visit www.stanford.edu/group/ncpi/unspecified/assessment_states/instruments.html (retrieved April 16, 2014).
- For a framework to help advisors in the medical field but adaptable to other fields as well, see Woods, Burgess, Kaminetzky, McNeill, Pinheiro, & Heflin, 2010).
- Carnegie Initiative on the doctorate website at http://gallery.carnegiefoundation.org/cid/cid/cid_collection.html shows efforts in six subject areas as to what various ongoing programs and innovations multiple universities are exploring to improve doctoral programs in terms of advising committees, advising and mentoring innovation, and advisor guidelines (retrieved April 16, 2014).

REFERENCES

Anderson, M., & Swazey, J. (1998). Reflections on the graduate student experience: An overview. In M. Anderson (Ed.), *The experience of being in graduate school: An exploration* (pp. 327–340). New Directions for Student Services, no. 101. Amherst, NY: Prometheus Books.

Austin, A., & McDaniels, M. (2006). Preparing the professoriat of the future: Graduate student socialization for faculty roles. In J. Smart (Ed.), *Higher education handbook of theory and research*, Volume 21, (pp. 397–456). Dordrecht, Netherlands: Springer.

Barres, B. (2013). How to pick a graduate advisor. *Neuron, 80*, 275–279.

Barrick, K., Clark, R., & Blaschek, L. (2006). Current and expected roles of graduate student faculty mentors. *NACTA Journal, 50*(1), 6–9.

Bennett, J. (1998). *College professionalism: The academy, individuation, and the common good.* Phoenix, AZ: Oryx Press.

Bowen, H., & Rudenstine, N. (1992). *In pursuit of the PhD.* Princeton, NJ: Princeton University Press.

Boyle, P., & Boice, B. (1995, November). *The structure of good beginnings: The early experiences of graduate students.* Paper presented at the annual meeting of the Association for the Study of Higher Education, New York. (ERIC Document Reproduction Service No. ED391 403)

Brackman, J., Nunez, A., & Basu, A. (2010). Effectiveness of a conflict resolution training program in changing graduate student style of managing conflict with faculty advisors. *Innovative Higher Education, 35*, 277–293.

Brown, R., & Krager, L. (1985). Ethical issues in graduate education: Faculty and student responsibilities. *Journal of Higher Education, 56*, 403–418.

Brubaker, J., & Rudy, W. (1997). *Higher education in transition* (4th ed.). New Brunswick, NJ: Transaction Publishers.

Cassuto, L. (Ed.) (2012). *Surviving your graduate school advisor*. Washington, DC: The Chronicle of Higher Education.

Crum, C., & Franklin, K. (2002, November). *An exploration of mentoring female graduate students in southern metropolitan universities*. Paper presented at the annual meeting of the Mid-South Educational Research Association, Chattanooga, TN. (ERIC Document Reproduction Service No. ED474 592)

Damrosch, D. (1995). *We scholars: Changing the culture of the university*. Cambridge, MA: Harvard University Press.

Egan, J. (1989). Graduate school and the self: A theoretical view of some negative effects of professional socialization. *Teaching Sociology, 17,* 200–207.

Ellis, E. (2001). The impact of race and gender on graduate school socialization, satisfaction with doctoral study, and commitment to degree completion. *The Western Journal of Black Studies, 25,* 30–45.

Everson, S.T. (2009). A professional doctorate in educational leadership: Saint Louis University's Ed.D. program. *Peabody Journal of Education, 84,* 86–99.

Faison, J. (1996, April). *The next generation: The mentoring of African American graduate students on predominantly white campuses*. Paper presented at the annual meeting of the American Educational Research Association, New York. (ERIC Document Reproduction Service No. ED401 344)

Ferreira, M. (2000). *The ideal advisor: Graduate science students' perspective*. (ERIC Document Reproduction Service No. ED441 681)

Ferrer de Valero, Y. (2001). Department factors affecting time-to-degree and completion rates of doctoral students at one-land grant research institution. *Journal of Higher Education, 72,* 341–367.

Geiger, R. (2007). Research, graduate education, and the ecology of American universities: An interpretive history. In H. Wechsler, L. Goodchild, & L. Eisenmann (Eds.), *The history of higher of education* (3rd ed.), (pp. 316–331). ASHE Reader series. Boston: Pearson Custom Publishing.

Harrison, E. (2012). Development and pilot testing of a faculty advisor evaluation questionnaire. *Journal of Nursing Education, 51,* 167–169.

Hermanowicz, J. (2005). Classifying universities and their departments: A social world perspective. *Journal of Higher Education, 76,* 26–55.

Jackson, M., & Scheel, M. (2013). Quality of master's education: A concern for counseling psychologists? *The Counseling Psychologist, 41,* 669–699.

Jenks, C., & Riesman, D. (1977). *The American revolution*. Chicago: University of Chicago Press.

Johnson-Bailey, J., Valentine, T., Cervero, R., & Bowles, T. (2009). Rooted in the soil: The social experiences of Black graduate students at a southern research university. *Journal of Higher Education, 80,* 178–203.

Knox, S., Schlosser, L., Pruitt, N., & Hill, C. (2006). A qualitative examination of graduate advising relationships: The advisor perspective. *Counseling Psychologist, 34,* 489–518.

Levin, E. (2008). Career preparation for doctoral students: The University of Kansas history department. In C. Colbeck, K. O'Meara, & A. Austin (Eds.), *Educating integrated professionals: Theory and practice on the preparation of the professoriat* (pp. 83–97). New Directions for Teaching and Learning, no. 113. San Francisco: Jossey-Bass.

Lovitts, B. (2001). *Leaving the ivory tower: The causes and consequences of departure from doctoral study*. Lanham, MD: Rowman-Littlefield.

Luebs, M., Fredrickson, K., Hyon, S., & Samraj, B. (1998). John Swales as mentor: The view from the doctoral group. *English for Specific Purposes, 17*, 67–85.

Marsh, H., Rowe, K., & Martin, A. (2002). PhD students' evaluation of research supervision. *Journal of Higher Education, 73*, 313–348.

Murdock, G. (1960). *Social structure*. New York: Macmillan.

Noy, S., & Ray, R. (2012). Graduate student perceptions of their advisors: Is there systematic disadvantage in mentorship? *Journal of Higher Education, 83*, 876–914.

O'Meara, K., Knudsen, K., & Jones, J. (2013). The role of emotional competency in faculty–doctoral student relationships. *Review of Higher Education, 36*, 315–347.

Parsons, T., & Platt, G. (1973). *The American university*. Cambridge, MA: Harvard University Press.

Rice, K., Choi, C., Zhang, Y., Villegas, J., Huen, J., Anderson, D., Nesic, A., & Bigler, M. (2009). International student perspectives on graduate advising relationships. *Journal of Counseling Psychology, 56,* 376–391.

Richardson, P., MacRae, A., Schwartz, K., Bankston, L., & Kosten, C. (2008). Student outcomes in a post-professional online masters'-degree program. *The American Journal of Occupational Therapy, 62*, 600–610.

Schlosser, L., & Kahn, J. (2007). Dyadic perspectives in advisor–advisee relationships in counseling psychology doctoral programs. *Journal of Counseling Psychology, 54*, 211–217.

Schlosser, L., Knox, S., Moskowitz, A., & Hill, C. (2003). A qualitative examination of graduate advising relationships: The advisee perspective. *Journal of Counseling Psychology, 50*, 178–188.

Schlosser, L., Lyons, H., Talleyrand, R., Kim, B., & Johnson, W.B. (2011a). A multicultural infused model of graduate advising relationships. *Journal of Career Development, 38*, 44–61.

Schlosser, L., Lyons, H., Talleyrand, R., Kim, B., & Johnson, W.B. (2011b). Advisor–advisee relationships in graduate training programs. *Journal of Career Development, 38*, 3–18.

Strauss, A. (1964). Regularized status-passage. In W. Bennis, E. Schein, D. Berlow, & F. Steele (Eds.), *Interpersonal dynamics* (pp. 409–416). Homewood, IL: Dorsey Press.

Sutton, K., & Sankar, C. (2011). Student satisfaction with information provided by academic advisors. *Journal of STEM Education, 12*(7/8), 71–86.

Tierney, W. (1997). Organizational socialization in higher education. *Journal of Higher Education, 68,* 1–16.

55

TWIG Writing Group. (1996). A feminist perspective on graduate student–advisor relationships. *Feminist Teacher, 10*, 17–25.

Walker, G., Golde, C., Jones, L., Bueschel, A., & Hutchings, P. (2008). *The formation of scholars.* San Francisco: Jossey-Bass.

Wolff, K. (1950). *The sociology of Georg Simmel.* Glencoe, IL: Free Press.

Woods, S., Burgess, L., Kaminetzky, C., McNeill, D., Pinheiro, S., & Heflin, M. (2010). Defining the role of advisors and mentors in post graduate medical education: Faculty perceptions, roles, responsibilities, and resource needs. *Journal of Graduate Medical Education, 2*, 195–200.

Wrench, J., & Punyanunt, N. (2004). Advisee–advisor communications: An exploratory study examining interpersonal communication variables in the graduate advisor–advisee relationship. *Communication Quarterly, 52*, 224–236.

Zhao, C., Golde, C., & McCormick, A. (2007). More than a signature: How advisor choice and advisor behavior affect doctoral student satisfaction. *Journal of Further and Higher Education, 31*, 263–281.

Chapter 5

Accounting for Differences

Advising Diverse Groups

According to the Council of Graduate School's (2008) report, graduate enrollment continues to rise by approximately 3% per year and more doctorates are awarded as new student populations pass through our graduate schools. Because of the varying experiences of male, female, younger, older, majority, minority, native, non-native, part-time, GLBT, disabled, and veteran graduate students across various programs, the validity of a one-size-fits-all advising model would not address all the specific needs of each student group and subdivisions with those groups studying in our disciplines and professions (Brus, 2006; Ellis, 2001). In addition, research provides conflicting outcomes associated with diversity which further affects and confounds advising. Helpful recommendations based on that research, however, provide advisors with suggestions and options to employ in their own advising.

GENDER

Doctoral student attrition among women occurred more frequently in the sciences and math but no clear reason existed to say whether the departure came from a philosophical disparity, a socio-cultural mismatch, or some other reason altogether (Herzig, 2004). Ferreira (2003) found that women described their chemistry department as cutthroat, where women were marginal, and the climate characterized as crude and competitive. Some women departed the program claiming advisor issues as the cause and offered indication that the environment proved unfriendly.

In their extensive study of PhD students, Nettles and Millett (2006) found men were more likely than women to choose an advisor or mentor of the same sex. Women preferred a female mentor more so than a female faculty advisor because cross-gender pairings resulted in different outcomes. While females are as likely as their male counterparts to receive similar treatment from advisors, fields with fewer female faculty advisors may be at a disadvantage compared to more balanced disciplines and professions (Schlosser, Lyons, Talleyrand, Kim, & Johnson, 2011b). This may be due to an implied power differential between opposite gender advisor/advisee relationships (Casto, Caldwell, & Salazar, 2005). Advisors who offer a more gender neutral advising approach toward women students served in a better capacity (Heinrich, 1990).

RACE/ETHNICITY

What a Pleasant Surprise

All of Professor Cassals' first-year master's advisees signed up for her history class. All of them worked on campus as graduate assistants and participated well in class. Following the first assignment grade, all but one of them did well. Quite surprised and disappointed by the outcome, the professor wondered how David would react when he saw his low grade. The next morning, an email came from David asking Cassals for her next available appointment. She anticipated the meeting would be tense and confrontational. When David arrived he thanked Cassals for her honesty in grading and appreciated her feedback and suggestions to improve his next paper. As her mouth gaped in astonishment, her heart filled with compassion. David explained that as an African-American student, he found professors danced around him giving him better grades than even he knew he deserved. It caused him to put less effort into his work because no matter what, his work never needed to reflect his true ability. He told Cassals that her comments indicated she cared about him and he would do his best to live up to her expectations.

Brown, Davis, and McClendon (1999) debunked sacred academic values and concluded that not every senior professor can effectively advise a graduate student, particularly a minority student. Advising students of color is different from advising non-minority students because of how this ultimately affects the faculty/student relationship and how faculty relates to students of color. In fact, faculty often establishes more isolation than they would with non-minority students (Davidson & Foster-Johnson, 2001; Schlemper & Monk, 2011). Clearly Professor Cassals experienced difficulty anticipating David's reaction to her written comments. She worried how her honesty would be received. Tense moments eventually turned into a more productive advisor/advisee relationship but cross-racial pairings do not always have a happy ending.

Adams (1993) attributed the guild aspect of the collegium as one reason for the precarious environment many minority graduate students enter. Typically, faculty tends to select advisees in a homo-social manner, that is, choosing students who are similar to them. The downside to advising students of color often involves following stereotypes. This causes students to be skeptical of advisors outside their race, which may be an unfounded assumption at best and a reality at worst. In this instance, Cassals seemed more skeptical of her advisee based on those stereotypes which could have been garnered from her own past experience. As such, cross-racial advising can affect a student's identity and professional development.

In the Willie, Grady, and Hope (1991) study, black students at predominantly white institutions indicated they experienced less access to faculty than white peers. Black students at another PWI "experienced discrimination, isolation, and loneliness" especially from the university community and within their graduate program and described their situation as "something they endured and survived" rather than fondly remembered (Johnson-Bailey, Valentine, Cervero, & Bowles, 2009, p. 192).

Faculty/student interaction cannot be overstated (Fountaine, 2011). Nettles (1990) indicated that black students experienced greater support from advisors and mentors than white students. While students needed to make same race connections during their time in the program, Barker (2011) noted that white faculty advisors could be effective but that these advisors should also encourage their advisees of color to make meaningful connections with same race peers, academics, support personnel, and practicing professionals to augment the primary cross-race advisor/advisee relationship.

In contrast to the PWI, the HBCU environment nurtures doctoral students with a supportive campus climate where students report a "high level of advisor engagement . . . and . . . were pleased with the amount and quality of time they spent with their advisor" (Fountaine, 2011, p. 142). Positive feelings emerged when interactions were academic as well as social. Partnerships between HBCUs and graduate programs at PWIs helped considerably to facilitate better advising and mentoring. In fact, much-needed support from the undergraduate HBCUs served to "demystify the process of reaching a PhD" for black students (Stassum, Sturm, Holly-Bockelman, Burger, Ernst, & Webb, 2011, p. 376). Furthermore, tracking student progress through bridge programs and matching the advisor and student who espoused the same research interests increased retention efforts.

Native American culture encompasses an interdependent component, connecting one person to another in a sense of mutual caring and respect rather than a hierarchical approach as would be found in a traditional advisor/advisee or master/apprentice relationship. Native American students expressed discomfort competing with their peers, for instance, on research teams for specific positions or for various types of rewards. Students tended to be "more sensitized to a lack of respect and to micro-aggressions and are in a very vulnerable position to be able to speak up in the moment" (Barcus & Crowley, 2012, p. 76). The cultural aversion to competing for a research position or arguing the merits of a thesis/dissertation proposal topic may appear to a faculty advisor/supervisor as student passivity, disinterest, or disengagement when in reality it is culturally shaped behavior.

Advisors of Native American students need to be more culturally aware of student necessaries to overcome social and cultural isolation. This can be accomplished by staying in close touch with Native American students and listening to them relay aspects of their culture. Faculty should provide opportunities for Native American students to work on their self-esteem and help with offering emotional support when needed. To ignore or fail to acknowledge their ideas or culture indicates faculty disinterest to students. As a result, students will be unlikely to bother the advisor again. Native American students need a solid advisor/advisee fit with someone willing to utilize their specific cultural attributes to enhance their progress in the graduate program (Barcus & Crowley, 2012; Tate & Schwartz, 1993).

Diversity factors further complicate advising and the student socialization process by forcing students to adjust to professional standards, behaviors, and attitudes as well as departmental norms. In the absence of departmentally introduced support groups, Latino and African-Americans lacking peer support groups met outside their academic department in order to create supportive environments for themselves and deal with the isolation they felt within the department. These groups emerged when black and Latino doctoral students began to self-censor their own words and actions and "question their self-efficacy, . . . [became] . . . stifled in their scholarly endeavors, and [relied] on peer support networks" stemming from what they called "a dehumanizing culture" (Gildersleeve, Croom, & Vasquez, 2011, p. 108). Faculty advisors need to be more aware of these situations and not presume that a self-initiated peer group formed for positive reasons only. Department chairs need to monitor the prevailing culture in their departments and find ways to promote inclusion. Peer mentoring can affect student integration and enculturation particularly for students of color and international students (Smailes & Gannon-Leary, 2011) but it needs to grow from intentional program objectives rather than grow out of feelings of isolation and oppression.

Gasman, Gerstl-Pepin, Anderson-Thompson, Rasheed, and Hathaway (2004) recommended that faculty collaboration with students may reveal some critical information about oppressive environments felt by minority graduate students. Situations where students cooperate in and collaborate with faculty for decision-making purposes in the student's program often tends to be a foreign experience for students (Caplow & Kardash, 1995) but one from which they can learn, contribute to their socialization into the profession, and make the journey to the degree a much more pleasant one.

RACE/ETHNICITY AND GENDER

The advisor/advisee or master/apprentice dynamic can be further exacerbated when race/ethnicity *and* gender factor in the equation. Men and women desire different qualities in a faculty advisor but race differences can marginalize students of color. As a result, minority groups and especially women and minority women experience greater perceived levels of isolation in their programs (Noy & Ray, 2012; Schlosser et al, 2011b). African-American women seeking advisors in PWIs struggled with the lack of a critical mass of same race, same sex faculty advisors, especially in the sciences versus education and the humanities (Grant & Simmons, 2008; Patton & Harper, 2003). As a result, students often seek out a second advisor who fulfills needs unmet by their primary advisor (Noy & Ray, 2012). This advisor/mentor may be an administrator, faculty from another department, or someone from off-campus. Guiding these students to add supplementary mentors of color should provide them with additional types of emotional and social support that complements the primary advisor/advisee relationship.

How faculty and students handle the inherent status differential in the relationship can be revealing (Braxton, Proper, & Bayer, 2011; Peluso, Carleton, Richter, & Asmundson, 2011). Recall that David rather than Professor Cassals set the tone for their relationship. This indicates that professional development for faculty on diversity issues and consciously acknowledging the differences in gender and cultural identity in cross-gender/cross-race relationships are strongly encouraged (Barker, 2011).

Awareness of cultural values can also aid advisors to assist cross-gender pairings and students of color with identity development as it relates to student professional development. For instance, Latina social work students felt a sense of ambivalence and submission within their own professional identity development. Specifically, integrating "a professional social work identity with the firmly embedded cultural value of serving others, anticipating needs, and submission proved challenging" for these women (Leyva, 2011, p. 27). Although the social work profession emphasized service to others, something expected of Latinas culturally, their submission caused them to not self-advocate when they needed to do that within their programs like David did with Professor Cassals.

GENERATIONAL DIFFERENCES

First-generation students tend to be as clueless about going to graduate school as they were about starting college. Because these students may not be savvy enough to guide themselves, faculty advisors need to be more vigilant about assessing and appraising their readiness, aptitude, and fitness for a particular graduate school or program. Should a student show promise, decisions need to be discussed regarding their geographic relocation, need for an assistantship, time-to-degree expectations, job prospects in the field, and application process and deadlines for materials. They may need additional information on program reputation, securing recommendations/endorsements, and fleshing out their initial research interests (Lunceford, 2011).

First-generation students may not recognize their potential and thus dismiss an opportunity to continue their schooling. Barbato, Story, Fritz, and Schinstock (2011) "indicated that advisors who gave personal attention to advisees, valued each student's individual needs and encouraged the students' continuous improvement" (p. 667). Individuation may be related positively to advisor effectiveness and satisfaction. Increasing candidate pools of first-generation students, especially students of color, can begin when faculty advisors identify promising undergraduates, interacting more frequently with them, motivating and stimulating them intellectually, and introducing them to research and scholarly writing and presenting.

The bulk of students in our graduate program now include Generation Y members born after 1982. Often called Millennials, these students are confident and entitled; sheltered and close to parents; and destination, achievement, and team-oriented. Millennials are extremely comfortable with technology and technological devices. In fact, technological communication is often preferable to face-to-face encounters. Research shows that Millennials "regularly seek out faculty for feedback and assurance," which takes up more faculty time and energy than did previous age cohorts of students (Rickes, 2009, p. 11). Unlike other graduate generations before them, Millennials expect orientations and continuous feedback, prefer to work collaboratively, and work best when they feel valued (Luscombe, Lewis, & Biggs, 2013). Millennials tend not to be interested in the serendipity of the graduate journey but rather its ultimate outcome, the credential and the job.

Nettles and Millett (2006) speculated on the current trend of student entitlement and lamented that students' needs, expectations, and often demands may well exist beyond faculty and department capabilities to fulfill. Millennials also experienced higher levels of stress and depression and other anxiety disorders. Advising Millennials may prove problematic to faculty and require the development of an advising style different from that needed in previous generations (Luscombe, Lewis, & Biggs, 2013). Faculty advisors should be aware of these generational student dispositions and seek information on how best to deal with them. Faculty advisors should solicit advice from the campus counseling center or encourage their Millennials to also seek counseling services when needed to address their higher levels of stress and anxiety.

SEXUAL ORIENTATION

Not My Area

Donald approached Professor Kidd with his proposed dissertation topic and he indicated that he wanted Kidd to chair it given her knowledge of the leadership literature. Kidd sat speechless when Donald revealed that he wanted to do a qualitative study on gays in higher educational leadership and issues related to whether the campus community accepted and valued their leadership abilities or discriminated against them. Clearly, Kidd had no idea Donald was gay. Donald showed Kidd a picture of his son and talked about Pat whom Kidd presumed was his wife. Pat was his partner and together they adopted and were raising their son. Although Kidd allowed Donald to tell her more about the topic and the methodology, Kidd told Donald she would have to think about it given her teaching, advising, research, and service load. Kidd's schedule could have accommodated Donald's research but, truthfully, she could not oversee a dissertation focusing on this particular topic. She was thrilled that Donald had asked her but she did not feel comfortable or competent enough to accept this challenge. At their next meeting, Kidd said that after having given it much thought, she could not add one more thing to her schedule. She suggested that another professor in the department whom Donald had for his research methods class would be perfect as the chair. Kidd had seen a rainbow symbol on Professor Lehner's door so she rationalized he would be delighted to be Donald's chair.

Gay, lesbian, bisexual, and transgender (GLBT) students may experience difficulties with their advisor. In some cases, the problem would not be described as open hostility but more of subtle indifference or lack of acceptance. Bias and discrimination still follow these students and Donald was no exception. As a result, many students seek out GLBT advisors in search of more supportive, affirming relationships, hence the display of a rainbow symbol on Lehner's door. Fortunately for Donald, Professor Lehner would probably be a better fit than Kidd. Reluctance to identify an advisor other than one who is GLBT stemmed from students' belief that faculty might not relate to sexual orientation issues in ways that furthered approachability, advocacy, nurturance, and authenticity (Schlosser et al, 2011b). While Donald may not have realized Kidd harbored resistance, he may not have had much choice in selection given that his leadership topic matched Kidd's research interests.

Furthermore, successful GLBT advising and student social identity development tends also to be contingent upon the prevailing campus culture and demographic factors within the university, department, and specific program as they related to GLBT students. Demographics may relate directly or indirectly to the socio-political culture and climate of the department. Therefore, care should be taken to ensure GLBT students are appreciated and supported when they search for chairs and committee members to oversee research related to GLBT issues.

If students intend to explore GLBT issues in the profession through their research, additional areas need to be considered as early as admission. Specifically, faculty needs to be able and willing to chair research topics in this area. Second, the necessity of research in GLBT areas could play a significant role in fields where a paucity of research exists, making these candidates highly attractive to the future of specific professions/disciplines (Schlosser et al, 2011b). Kidd missed a prime opportunity to supervise research that dealt with cutting-edge issues as well as learning more about Donald's life style and how as the qualitative researcher it informs his findings. However, Kidd assessed her skills as lacking in this topic area and chose to pass Donald to a colleague who she anticipated better understood and sympathized with GLBT issues.

INTERNATIONAL STUDENTS

With over one half million international students studying in American universities alone, many serving as graduate assistants, faculty encounter opportunities to advise and supervise students from different cultural regions. While these students bring advantages to the learning environment, they also challenge university administrators and faculty advisors to address unique international student needs and expectations in ways native students do not (Trice, 2003).

Dong (1998) did a comparison of faculty advisors and their native and non-native science and engineering dissertation students. Faculty believed they offered more of their time to students than students estimated they did. Dong noted that academic dishonesty also occurred more often among non-native than native doctoral students, who in addition to language difficulties did not always recognize plagiarism. In addition, language barriers hampered students' writing but students noted that their faculty advisors provided only limited assistance. Dissertation students recalled their advisors gave little feedback in terms of topic, problem statement, and research development when in fact these students required more from their advisors.

Furthermore, faculty advisors need to also be aware that the translation of words from other languages into English is not the only concern. Other languages honor different writing styles and traditions, of which some emphasize flowery, descriptive language more than others, which emphasize more logic. Concise versus precise language may confound the technical style of writing common to theses/dissertations (Dong, 1998).

Faculty expected less from non-native speakers than native ones in terms of draft revisions. Ironically, more revisions would have helped improve non-native students' writing style. Non-native students subsequently reported less involvement in scholarly publication than native speakers, further placing these students at a professional disadvantage. As a result, non-native students felt isolated, having little contact with their advisors and native peers but relying instead on other international students for help and support (Dong, 1998).

Curtin, Stewart, and Ostrove (2013) compared international and native graduate students to learn more about the extent to which advisor support affected student self-concept. Good advisor/advisee relationships cultivate students' "sense of belonging and academic self-concept . . . [including] . . .

64

facilitating students' positive beliefs about themselves as academics" (p. 112). Advisor support related to positive self-concept and sense of belonging for native as well as international students. Participants described belonging as the presence of a welcoming, respectful, pragmatic environment. Self-concept included the sense of encouragement, confidence, and performance. In other words, self-concept meant "doing well" and sense of belonging meant "fitting-in" for native students but not for international students. Curtin et al concluded "that because international students attach more importance to research and professional-related experiences, they felt they fit in well with the academic environment despite their social isolation from peers" (p. 130). Advisor tool kits need additional resources to assist with international student needs.

Double Jeopardy

Admission to the fall master's cohort included a female student from Russia and another from India. Anya lived with her husband, attended class full time, and held a part-time position at a local community college because she was unable to secure an assistantship on campus. Sharma had an assistantship on campus and lived alone but nearby to the man her family back in India had arranged for her to marry. They frequently sought academic, work (Anya), and personal (Sharma) advice from their female advisor, Professor Markham. She did her best to fulfill academic needs but struggled with the work/personal/cultural issues. Anya experienced multiple issues with her lab supervisor which often jeopardized her continuation in the part-time position. Apparently things Anya shared in Markham's administration class were leaked to her supervisor by Lynn, another student in Anya's class. Sharma, who did well in class, experienced anxiety associated with finishing her degree because when she did she would have to marry Sanjay and return to India. Living away from her native country and working and studying with many American female students, Sharma wanted affirmation from Markham that taking a position in the United States after graduation would be the better option because she was not in love with her betrothed. Markham struggled to tell Anya how to confront Lynn and reminded the administration class again that what was said there, stayed there. While she wanted to grant Sharma her freedom and give her a great letter of recommendation for a job at an American university, Markham had no idea if culturally that was the best direction for Sharma to take.

Diversity affects interpersonal relations in the advisor/advisee dyad. Advising international students increases faculty's need for more cultural information and often requires sensitivity training as well. To further complicate matters, international students may not understand the role of faculty advisor and/or their role as advisee in the academic cultural context, especially with regard to expectations for either party or the subtle nuances of the American graduate educational system (Knox, Sokol, Inman, Schlosser, Nilsson, & Wang, 2013). Professor Markham found herself in a precarious position wanting to help Anya and Sharma but not really knowing where to begin. In a larger program or school that caters to a broad spectrum of international students, she might have checked with international alumni or international faculty across campus or campus student groups about how to better serve a particular international ethnicity or religious group (Trice, 2003).

In addition, faculty may harbor cultural stereotypes and biases they need to address before being able to assist their international advisees. Trice (2003) learned that faculty characterized international students based on what they observed about them and that, in turn, affected how the advisor and the departments responded to them. Ironically, the faculty had a tendency to view all graduate students either native or non-native the same, but simultaneously realized the international graduate students faced issues of both an academic and a personal nature. Markham could have obtained information from the campus office of international student services and found time for opportunities to attend workshops and seminars on cultural integration (Trice, 2003).

Chances for cultural conflicts may arise as a result of expectations of the field in which the student studies. These can stall student adjustment to the graduate student role as well as affect the student's emotional disposition. Students may be expecting more social and emotional support and cultural understanding from faculty advisors as well as greater faculty availability (Knox et al, 2013). Sharma and Anya looked to Markham for more emotional support not always realizing that she, too, needed to lean on others at the university for assistance in dealing with these issues. International students may fare best if matched to faculty with similar research interests as well as with faculty who share their ethnicity, who have extensive international travel experience or study abroad experiences, and/or who display greater cultural sensitivity (Knox et al, 2013).

PART-TIME STATUS AND WORK/LIFE BALANCE

In an online course discussion post, a graduate student described her part-time status as feeling like a "shadow that pops in and out of classrooms at odd times" (Amy Lavallee, University of Pittsburgh, March 28, 2014). According to Neumann and Rodwell (2009), "part-time students have fewer opportunities to be present in their departments during their [candidacy] to utilize the infrastructure resources available, or to participate in the research culture of the departments" (p. 59). Part-time students interact less frequently with their faculty advisor even before candidacy but realize significantly the lack of contact after completing coursework. These students remain at a disadvantage to their full-time student counterparts whose on-campus presence affords them benefits part-time students have little time to realize (Brubaker & Rudy, 1997; Ryan, 1973). Part-time students spend limited time on campus, lessening academic department visibility and leading to fewer opportunities for advising, formal or informal mentoring, or networking opportunities. These students often feel marginalized and stop out of their programs, often jeopardizing their chances to complete the degree. As a result, faculty advisors may place a decreased investment in part-time students because they have lowered expectations for their finishing their programs (Brus, 2006). When faculty admits full-time *and* part-time students, they owe them the same quality of advising.

Work/life balance issues such as part-time status, non-traditional age, family pressures, work demands, and single parenthood create more advising challenges for faculty. Advisors would be wise to schedule in advance more semester face-to-face or virtual meetings with these students and phone or email them more frequently to maintain a social support connection. Faculty is encouraged to know their advisees' most pressing issues and deal with any problems before they transform into major obstacles. In other words, advisors need to be aware of what work/life balance issues affect a student's degree program participation. Academic departments may reach out to student affairs personnel in order to connect students to available campus programs and resources beyond the purview of the department or the faculty advisor (Brus, 2006).

DISCIPLINARY DIFFERENCES

Definitions of student success in doctoral education vary by discipline/field, especially considering that each discipline/field upholds expectations and values for its students either as candidates for admission or candidates for the degree. Agriculture and education faculty, for example, regarded academic advisement of primary importance to graduate students, especially planning the degree program and maintaining frequent contact with students (Timko, Linhardt, & Stewart, 1991). Other departments may place less emphasis on this and devote more to something else. For instance, some departments placed paramount value on conference presentation, collaboration, publishing, teaching, or grant writing. Faculty in these departments role model and deliberately encourage these skills (Peluso et al, 2011) and push for student self-direction toward the professional goals of publication, post-doctoral fellowships, and academic job placement (Gardner, 2009).

Slawski (1973) concluded that the social distance between advisor and advisee differs by discipline/field. For instance, mechanical engineers practicing a hard applied science maintain lower social distance than cliquish, group-oriented anthropologists engaged in the softer sciences. By contrast, some disciplinary cultures Gardner (2009) found exuded a team spirit and a genuine caring for students. Disciplines and departments maintain their own esprit de corps, emphasize different aspects, and socialize and professionalize to that end (Weidman, Twale, & Stein, 2001).

Levin (2008) posited that faculty advisors supervise advisees following their *own* individual style, which may or may not be effective based on student demographics or discipline/field. Because good advising is critical to student success, advising teams could offer students exposure to multiple styles and assist faculty in learning additional advising approaches. Often interdisciplinary and cross-disciplinary interaction offers challenges that provide learning opportunities for advisors.

VETERANS

Faculty may also advise (face-to-face and online) active duty service personnel, reservists, veterans, disabled veterans, and career officers planning ahead for a profession beyond military retirement. Coming from a military culture into an academic culture, these groups may have their own specific needs and expectations of faculty of which advisors need to be cognizant. Faculty need to be aware of special online services like web conferencing that can be provided to students suddenly called to duty. Faculty may also need specific help and information from the campus office of veterans' services to assist with advising. These graduate students may require more flexible timelines and scheduling as well as additional special needs and accommodations. Returning veterans may need additional counseling and student support services (Ford, Northrup, & Wiley, 2009) within as well as outside faculty purview.

Retiring officers may require thorough pre-admission counseling from faculty as to the differences in academic and military culture and faculty's academic program expectations. Transferability of military skills to civilian positions and job prospects in any field is an essential discussion faculty must schedule prior to admission. Service personnel may also wish to use their unique military perspectives to incorporate into their research and coursework (Ford et al, 2009). Aligning these with a specific discipline/field, student's abilities, thesis/dissertation topics, and career goals encourage laudable student risk taking but also raise unique advising challenges.

GRADUATE STUDENTS WITH DISABILITIES

Information guiding faculty response to students with disabilities abounds on college campuses. This information has become a staple of course syllabi. In most disciplines/fields, physical disabilities pose little or no concern to degree completion. However, certain physical disabilities may prevent students from accomplishing tasks in some of the health areas where dexterity is required.

Reichgott (1998) reminded us that "if carefully selected and supported, a significantly disabled student *can* succeed in a rigorous medical school system" (p. 79). As a result, all programs should have guidelines in place to assist faculty with special advising needs of students with disabilities admitted to those programs. Faculty may need to make necessary accommodations and adjustments with regard to off-campus placements in internships, clinical, or practicum situations.

BEST PRACTICES

- More research on diversity is needed to advise students in each of these groups more effectively. Faculty advisors and disciplines/fields should support dissertation research on issues related to all these diverse groups and their uniqueness (Pruitt & Isaac, 1985).
- Faculty advisors need to recognize the antiquity of the one-size-fits-all advising model and accept that their information and advising style will need to be updated and broadened to address the needs of a diverse graduate student population. Seminars for advisors should focus on the role of student cultural and social identity in the advising and thesis/dissertation chairing process (Schlosser, Lyons, Talleyrand, Kim, & Johnson, 2011a). Diversity training programs should be assessed periodically to determine their value to advisors and supervisors (Knox, Schlosser, Pruitt, & Hill, 2006).
- Faculty should avoid stereotyping student groups as difficult to advise. Advisees must be viewed as unique individuals (Noy & Ray, 2012). Departments must exude a welcoming attitude and structure a socially, academically, and physically welcoming environment for all types of students. Students' need for belonging portends retention, whereas feelings of marginality encourage student disengagement and/or departure (Austin & McDaniels, 2006).

RESOURCES

- Each campus has offices focusing on diversity, disability, international, and veterans issues. Faculty should take advantage of professional development opportunities for advisors, supervisors, and chairs working with diverse student populations.
- Faculty advisors should guide students to association websites in search of doctoral fellowship and grant opportunities important to underrepresented student groups seeking to conduct research on issues related to diverse student groups. The American Educational Research Association offers minority students opportunities at www.aera.net/ProfessionalOpportunitiesFunding/AERAFundingOpportunities/ AERAMinorityDissertationFellowshipPrograminEducationResearch/tabid/10243/ Default.aspx as does the Society for the Study of Social Problems at www. ssspl.org/index.cfm/m/261/racial/ethnic_minority_graduate_scholarship/. Specific disciplines/fields may have similar opportunities.

69

■ International Statistical Institute website located at www.isi-web.org/ offers information on international student programs.

REFERENCES

Adams, H. (1993). *Focusing on the campus milieu: A guide for enhancing the graduate school climate*. Notre Dame University: National Center for the Graduation of Minorities. (ERIC Document Reproduction Service No. ED381 065)

Austin, A., & McDaniels, M. (2006). Preparing the professoriat of the future: Graduate student socialization for faculty roles. In J. Smart (Ed.), *Higher education handbook of theory and research*, Volume 21 (pp. 397–456). Dordrecht, Netherlands: Springer.

Barbato, J., Story, J., Fritz, S., & Schinstock, J. (2011). Full range advising: Transforming the advisor–advisee experience. *Journal of College Student Development*, *52*, 656–670.

Barcus, C., & Crowley, S. (2012). Training ethnic minority graduate students in a white man's program: Don't get bucked off! *Journal of Multicultural Counseling and Development*, *40*(2), 70–81.

Barker, M. (2011). Racial context, currency, and connections: Black doctoral students and while advisors' perspectives on cross-race advising. *Innovation in Education and Teaching International*, *48*, 387–400.

Braxton, J., Proper, E., & Bayer, A. (2011). *Professors behaving badly*. Baltimore: Johns Hopkins University Press.

Brown, M., Davis, G., & McClendon, S. (1999). Mentoring graduate students of color: Myths, models, and modes. *Peabody Journal of Education*, *74*, 105–118.

Brubaker, J., & Rudy, W. (1997). *Higher education in transition* (4th ed.). New Brunswick, NJ: Transaction Publishers.

Brus, C. (2006). Seeking balance in graduate school: A realistic expectation or dangerous dilemma? In M. Guentzel, & B. Nesheim, (Eds.), *Supporting graduate and professional students: The role of student affairs* (pp. 31–45). New Directions for Student Services, no. 115. San Francisco: Jossey-Bass.

Caplow, J., & Kardash, C. (1995). Collaborative learning activities in graduate courses. *Innovative Higher Education*, *19*, 207–222.

Casto, C., Caldwell, C., & Salazar, C. (2005). Creating mentoring relationships between female faculty and students in counselor education: Guidelines for potential mentees and mentors. *Journal of Counseling & Development*, *83*, 331–336.

Council of Graduate Schools. (2008). 2008 Reports. Washington, DC: Council of Graduate Schools. www.cgsnet.org/benchmarking/reports/2008-reports.

Curtin, N., Stewart, A., & Ostrove, J. (2013). Fostering academic self-concept: Advisor support and sense of belonging among international and domestic graduate students. *American Educational Research Journal*, *50*, 108–137.

Davidson, M., & Foster-Johnson, L. (2001). Mentoring in the preparation of graduate researchers of color. *Review of Educational Research*, *71*, 549–574.

Dong, Y. (1998). Non-native graduate students' thesis/dissertation writing in science: Self-reports by students and their advisors from two U.S. institutions. *English for Specific Purposes, 17*, 369–390.

Ellis, E. (2001). The impact of race and gender on graduate school socialization, satisfaction with doctoral study, and commitment to degree completion. *The Western Journal of Black Studies, 25*, 30–45.

Ferreira, M. (2003). Gender issues related to graduate student attrition in two science departments. *International Journal of Science in Education, 25*, 969–989.

Ford, D., Northrup, P., & Wiley, L. (2009). Connections, partnerships, opportunities, and programs to enhance success for military students. In R. Ackerman, & D. Di Ramio (Eds.), *Creating a veteran friendly campus: Strategies for transition and success* (pp. 61–69). New Directions for Student Services no. 126. San Francisco: Jossey-Bass.

Fountaine, T. (2011). The impact of faculty–student interaction on Black doctoral students attending historically Black institutions. *Journal of Negro Education, 81*, 136–147.

Gardner, S. (2009). Conceptualizing success in doctoral education: Perspectives of faculty in seven disciplines. *Review of Higher Education, 32*, 383–406.

Gasman, M., Gerstl-Pepin, C., Anderson-Thompson, S., Rasheed, L., & Hathaway, K. (2004). Negotiating power, developing trust: Transgressing race and status in the academy. *Teachers College Record, 106*, 689–715.

Gildersleeve, R., Croom, N., & Vasquez, P. (2011). "Am I going crazy?": A critical race analysis of doctoral education. *Equity and Excellence in Education, 44*, 93–114.

Grant, C., & Simmons, J. (2008). Narratives on experiences of African-American women in the academy: Conceptualizing effective mentoring relationships of doctoral students and faculty. *International Journal of Qualitative Studies in Education, 21*, 501–517.

Heinrich, K. (1990). *Toward gender sensitive advertisement of women doctoral students.* (ERIC Document Reproduction Service No. ED331 396)

Herzig, A. (2004). Becoming mathematicians: Women and students of color choosing and leaving doctoral mathematics. *Review of Educational Research, 72*, 171–214.

Johnson-Bailey, J., Valentine, T., Cervero, R., & Bowles, T. (2009). Rooted in the soil: The social experiences of Black graduate students at a southern research university. *Journal of Higher Education, 80*, 178–203.

Knox, S., Schlosser, L., Pruitt, N., & Hill, C. (2006). A qualitative examination of graduate advising relationships: The advisor perspective. *Counseling Psychologist, 34*, 489–518.

Knox, S., Sokol, J., Inman, A., Schlosser, L., Nilsson, J., & Wang, Y. (2013). International advisees' perspectives on the advising role in counseling doctoral programs. *International Perspectives on Psychology: Research, Practice, and Consultation, 2*(1), 45–61.

Levin, E. (2008). Career preparation for doctoral students: The University of Kansas history department. In C. Colbeck, K. O'Meara, & A. Austin (Eds.), *Educating integrated professionals: Theory and practice on the preparation of the professoriat* (pp. 83–97). New Directions for Teaching and Learning, no. 113. San Francisco: Jossey-Bass.

Leyva, V. (2011). First generation Latina graduate students: Balancing professional identity development with traditional family roles. In V. Harvey, & T. Housel (Eds.), *Faculty and first-generation college students: Bridging the classroom gap together* (pp. 21–31). New Directions for Teaching and Learning, no. 127. Hoboken, NJ: Wiley Periodicals Inc.

Lunceford, B. (2011). When first-generation students go to graduate school. In V. Harvey, & T. Housel (Eds.), *Faculty and first-generation college students: Bridging the classroom gap together* (pp. 13–20). New Directions for Teaching and Learning, no. 127. Hoboken, NJ: Wiley Periodicals Inc.

Luscombe, J., Lewis, I., & Biggs, H. (2013). Essential elements for recruitment and retention: Generation Y. *Education and Training, 55,* 272–290.

Nettles, M. (1990). *Black, Hispanic, and White doctoral students: Before, during, and after enrolling in graduate school.* Princeton, NJ: Educational Testing Service, Graduate Record Examination Board. (ERIC Document Reproduction Service No. ED406 947)

Nettles, M., & Millett, C. (2006). *Three magic letters: Getting the Ph.D.* Baltimore: Johns Hopkins University Press.

Neumann, R., & Rodwell, J. (2009). The "invisible" part-time research students: A case study of satisfaction and completion. *Studies in Higher Education, 34,* 55–68.

Noy, S., & Ray, R. (2012). Graduate student perceptions of their advisors: Is there systematic disadvantage in mentorship? *Journal of Higher Education, 83,* 876–914.

Patton, L., & Harper, S. (2003). Mentoring relationships among African-American women in graduate and professional schools. In M. Howard-Hamilton (Ed.), *Meeting the needs of African-American women* (pp. 67–78). New Directions for Student Services no. 104. San Francisco: Jossey-Bass.

Peluso, D., Carleton, N., Richter, A., & Asmundson, G. (2011). The graduate advising relationship in Canadian psychology programmes: Advisee perspectives. *Canadian Psychology, 52,* 29–40.

Pruitt, A., & Isaac, P. (1985). Discrimination in recruitment, admission, and retention of minority graduate students. *Journal of Negro Education, 54,* 526–536.

Reichgott, M. (1998). The disabled student as undifferentiated graduate: A medical school challenge. *JAMA, 279,* 79.

Rickes, P. (2009). Make way for the Millenials! How today's students are shaping higher education space: From generations on perspectives, through generational cycles, on to the influence of Millenials on campus space. *Planning for Higher Education, 37*(2), 7–17.

Ryan, J. (Ed.) (1973, December). Proceedings of the annual meeting of the Council of Graduate Schools in the United States, Williamsburg, VA. Washington, DC: Council of Graduate Schools in the United States. (ERIC Document Reproduction Service No. ED142 161)

Schlemper, M.B., & Monk, J. (2011). Discourses on "diversity": Perspectives from graduate programs in geography in the United States. *Journal of Geography in Higher Education, 35,* 23–46.

Schlosser, L., Lyons, H., Talleyrand, R., Kim, B., & Johnson, W.B. (2011a). A multicultural infused model of graduate advising relationships. *Journal of Career Development*, *38*, 44–61.

Schlosser, L., Lyons, H., Talleyrand, R., Kim, B., & Johnson, W.B. (2011b). Multicultural issues in graduate advising relationships. *Journal of Career Development*, *38*, 19–43.

Slawski, C. (1973, August). *Personal socialization in organizational context: Hypotheses and comparative cases.* Paper presented at the annual meeting of the American Psychological Association, New York. (ERIC Document Reproduction Service No. ED157 451)

Smailes, J., & Gannon-Leary, P. (2011). Peer mentoring—Is a virtual form of support a viable alternative? *Research in Learning Technology*, *19*, 129–142.

Stassum, K., Sturm, S., Holly-Bockelman, K., Burger, A., Ernst, D., & Webb, D. (2011). The Fisk-Vanderbilt Maser's-to-PhD Bridge Program: Recognizing, enlisting, and cultivating unrealized or unrecognized potential in underrepresented minority students. *American Journal of Physics*, *79*, 374–379.

Tate, D., & Schwartz, C. (1993). Increasing the retention of American Indian students in professional programs in higher education. *Journal of American Indian Education*, *33*(1), 21–31.

Timko, J., Linhardt, R., & Stewart, B. (1991). Educational needs of international graduate students in agriculture and education as perceived by University of Missouri-Columbia graduate faculty. *Journal of Agricultural Education*, *32*(4), 44–51.

Trice, A. (2003). Faculty perceptions of graduate international students: The benefits and challenges. *Journal of Studies in International Education*, *7*(4), 379–406.

Weidman, J., Twale, D., & Stein, E. (2001). *Socialization of graduate and professional students in higher education: A perilous passage?* San Francisco: Jossey-Bass.

Willie, C., Grady, M., & Hope, R. (1991). *African-Americans and the doctoral experience: Implications for policy.* New York: Teachers College Press.

Chapter 6

Supervising the Future

Assistantships, Clinicals, Internships, and Practicums

Faculty and students accrue benefits associated with supervision. Border and Barba (1998) found that students with assistantships and fellowships finished their program sooner and received helpful skills that led to a richer graduate school experience than did students who held neither of these positions during their graduate program. Supervising teaching assistants (TAs) and fellows, research assistants (RAs), or those completing internships, practicums, and clinical rotations requires additional faculty skills beyond advising. Evaluating the student as worker poses additional challenges. A practicum, internship, assistantship, or clinical residency offers supervisors opportunities for corrective intervention to aid students in perfecting professional practice. Graduate assistants (GAs) may be hired to perform tasks they typically did not perform previously and may require faculty and staff to supervise them in areas with which they are unfamiliar. Because students occupy these positions short term they pose distractions on the one hand while infusing new blood into the system on the other and require faculty to readjust and readapt quickly (White & Nonnamaker, 2011). In all situations, supervision demands mutual respect, open communication, frequent and constructive feedback, and regular time commitments by both parties (Walker, Golde, Jones, Bueschel, & Hutchings, 2008). This chapter examines the intricacies, expectations, power imbalances, and realities of supervising graduate students outside of the classroom and the importance of evaluation and ethical standards in that supervision.

GRADUATE TRAINING OPTIONS

As president of Johns Hopkins, Daniel Coit Gilman realized that a university's greatness rested on the character of its faculty and their research, not the aesthetics of its bricks and mortar. However, the difficulty in building a strong research university rested on attracting good faculty as well as post-baccalaureate students.

Land grant campus extension services provided a rich opportunity for apprentice graduate assistants to conduct research with faculty experts and receive financial support while completing their coursework (Brubaker & Rudy, 1997). In the mid-1870s, Harvard introduced the graduate fellowship concept which took several forms (Geiger, 2007, p. 321): post-residency specialty training in the medical fields; a non-tenure track visiting professorship; pre- or post-doctoral researcher; and a graduate-level, merit-based scholarship without work expectations.

Graduate education grew tremendously after World War II (White & Nonnamaker, 2011). Beginning in the 1970s, teaching assistantships proliferated to accommodate increases in undergraduate arts and sciences majors (Bowen & Rudenstine, 1992). By the mid-1980s, TAs covered more classes than ever before and rendered themselves a powerful underclass of "professionals" that offered financial relief to their institutions (Jenks & Riesman, 1977). Unfortunately, men filled more graduate assistantships than women, especially research assistantships (Syverson, 1982; Wong & Sanders, 1983).

To comprehend their intended profession, graduate students need to immerse themselves in the scholarly research of their discipline through internship and practicum opportunities indicative of the apprenticeship model (Jenks & Riesman, 1977). Internships can be paid/unpaid, credit/non-credit, temporary, short-term training periods supervised by faculty and onsite personnel designed to apply classroom-derived skills to real-world situations. Similarly, practicums allow for faculty-supervised student application of a previously learned theory, construct, or principle often in professional work settings. Many disciplines and all professional programs require or recommend students avail themselves of internship or practicum opportunities. To further student needs and apprentice future practitioners, other campus offices have begun to employ the services of graduate students. To supply temporary or short-term employment needs, graduate students accept assistantships in such areas as resident hall director, academic counselor, athletic trainer, and departmental "gopher" who serves an all-purpose function (White & Nonnamaker, 2011).

Students may hold a preceptorship in preparation for careers in medicine and nursing. Preceptors serve as skilled practitioners who supervise graduate student preceptorships. These students gain practical experience overseeing patients in a clinical setting (Luhanga, Yonge, & Myrick, 2008). Similarly, the clinical allows students under site supervision to observe and treat patients in hospital settings. Residency implies further mandatory post-internship medical training beyond the internship in a hospital setting. They encompass three to seven years of additional hospital experience designed for in-depth training in subspecialties but under the watchful eye of one or more practicing medical professionals (Woods, Burgess, Kaminetzky, McNeill, Pinheiro, & Heflin, 2010).

75

REALITIES OF FACULTY SUPERVISION

As important as the advisor/advisee relationship is to student success in the program, so too is supervisor/supervisee in the office, lab, classroom, or clinic (Smeby, 2000). Supervisors can act in one of several ways: (a) very paternalistic, bestowing and withholding approval; (b) midwives, delivering and bringing student ideas to life; (c) sergeants in boot camp, despotic and overbearing; (d) bubbly cheerleaders, championing students to victory; (e) laissez-faire managers, leaving students to flounder; or (f) coaches, instilling confidence to persevere (Buraway, 2005). Each of these options holds implications for how supervisors relate to their supervisees.

TA training has been described as mandatory, limited, varied, haphazard, inconsistent, and/or optional. Concomitantly, TA supervision varied similarly due to non-existent classroom observation by faculty supervisors (Buerkel-Rothfus & Gray, 1990; Prieto & Scheel, 2008). Supervising an RA by contrast means faculty should "create opportunities for graduate students to demonstrate their research prowess and to publish" (Braxton, Proper, & Bayer, 2011, p. 128). In addition, off-site practitioners and clinical supervisors must provide work-related direction and feedback to students if the experience is to be relevant to their future profession.

Supervisee "duties should be reasonable, specific to the person, and at best, contribute importantly to the program of studies and future career goals" (Madsen, 2003, p. 76). In reality, however, this may not always happen due to supervisor/supervisee imbalances of power.

DEALING WITH POWER IMBALANCES

Supervisors serve as employers, role models, and advisors/mentors acting in a fiduciary capacity. The key becomes *how* faculty plays out these roles while dealing with the students they supervise.

Because of the power relationship inherent in the supervisor/supervisee association, boundaries need to be established to reduce supervisee vulnerability as well as supervisor culpability and circumstances that render the reverse situation possible. The faculty supervisor may also serve as the student's professor and/or dissertation chair. These multiple encounters increase risk for power struggles and boundary crossing by both parties. Faculty and administration must uphold an ethical code and a professional departmental climate/culture that emphasizes the duties and boundaries of faculty's fiduciary responsibility. Supervisors, staff, and administration must also make certain that students understand the ethical code and expectations and boundaries of the relationship as well as be alert to the risks and consequences of crossing them (Chiang, 2009; Gottlieb, Robinson, & Younggren, 2007).

76

While instilling professional propriety may be the goal, supervisor/supervisee interaction often takes on a more personal relationship. While this may not be problematic in all professional and disciplinary areas, it could be awkward in the counseling fields. Biaggio, Paget, and Chenoweth (1997) asked how much should faculty and students disclose to one another beyond their academic relationship. Faculty must be vigilant not to counsel students in *the therapist* role but rather remain in the role of supervisor. When supervisor and supervisee cause each other emotional distress, the relationship has crossed a boundary and the issues must be resolved or the relationship terminated.

Professional codes of conduct and university policy should reflect boundary identification and its maintenance along with ways to prevent and resolve these events. Faculty and students need to be candid with each other to help prevent boundary crossings when they have the potential to occur. Biaggio et al (1997) indicated that faculty "bear responsibility for maintaining ethical relationships with students, and it is therefore incumbent on faculty to explicitly acknowledge their power over students" (pp. 86–87). In the midst of confusion, supervisees should seek clarification of the guidelines from supervisors, peers, advisors, university ombudspersons, or department/graduate school administrators.

Power imbalances also occur between master's and doctoral students working in the same classroom or lab setting. In Scarborough, Bernard, and Morse's (2006) study of counseling students, the imbalance of power between master's and doctoral students caused confusion as to how the two groups should interact with one another. In lab situations, doctoral students may be given authority over master's students. Faculty supervisors must apprise their doctoral students of proper expected behavior of each group and the boundaries not to be crossed that would jeopardize personal and social relationships, their research, professionalism, ethical codes, departmental/school policy, and student continuance in the graduate program or work situation. Scarborough et al suggested that guidelines should be contained in the graduate student handbook and/or included in an orientation session.

EXPECTATIONS OF FACULTY SUPERVISION

Supervision implies direct oversight of a student regardless of the venue: clinic, lab, classroom, or office. The goal is to promote the development of the students' teaching, research, clinical, and/or pre-professional skills. Goodyear, Crego, and Johnston (1992) offered eight categories of supervision of which six apply here. Supervisors must (1) be competent in subject area and research methods and statistics; (2) adequately perform duties; (3) be faithful in fulfilling the work contract; (4) be objective in their values and beliefs; (5) be helpful; and (6) be interactive rather than solitary. They recommended that policies exist to clearly address these areas with regard to supervisor/supervisee expectations.

77

Supervision also entails intervention to set supervisees on the correct path, remediate skill deficiencies, recommend personal counseling, or counsel them out of the position or program (Baltimore, 1998). For instance, working relationships with faculty supervisors in the dental school proved important "because supervisors' ongoing encouragement and support increased [student] self-confidence and facilitated learning" (Subramanian, Anderson, Morgaine, & Thompson, 2013). As a result, faculty support and approachability increased.

Often what students receive from supervised experiences can be traced back directly to the supervisor's goals and objectives (Granello, 2000). If faculty expects that students meet only basic cognitive objectives like knowledge, comprehension, and application, then supervisors may be shortchanging students. Faculty should consider designing supervisory experiences that aim for integration, application, and synthesis (Bloom, Engelhart, Furst, Hill, & Krathwohl, 1984; Krathwohl, Bloom, & Masia, 1964). Ideally students new to supervised experiences would need to master and demonstrate basic cognitive objectives before engaging in the upper levels of Bloom's Taxonomy. However, it would ensure that supervisors demonstrate greater organization and intent to developing supervisee skills.

Guided questioning, activities, new formats, and deliverables can be used to meet those objectives. Team supervisory models can help novice supervisors learn from seasoned supervisors how to take the student from lower- to higher-level objectives (Granello, 2000). Exploring Bloom's affective domain requires students to focus on valuing, appreciating, organizing, and internalizing (Krathwohl et al, 1964). For some professional areas like the health sciences, students routinely must demonstrate their psychomotor abilities in order to graduate. Bloom's Taxonomy can be a valuable tool for helping supervisors design learning objectives from all three domains for practica, clinicals, and internships as well as assistantships.

SUPERVISING MINORITY AND NON-NATIVE STUDENTS

Leave Well Enough Alone

In the fall semester, the department chair assigned Professor Campbell a new graduate assistant, LaToya. She was a mature and personable doctoral student with work experience. Campbell looked forward to working on a new research project and bringing LaToya into the process. The new associate dean, Jefferies, informed Campbell that in the winter semester he needed a graduate assistant and he felt LaToya, a minority student, would be the ideal choice. Luis, a doctoral student from another department would be assigned to Campbell. During the semester, Campbell could not enlist Luis in the research project. Luis told Campbell that the research tasks he had been assigned were beneath him and that he was better suited to teaching not research. When

Campbell went to relay the disappointing information to Jefferies, Jefferies asked her just how well LaToya had performed on the research project. "Just fine," Campbell replied. Apparently, LaToya did not acclimate well to the tasks expected of her in the dean's office, greatly disappointing Jefferies.

International graduate students rely on faculty supervisors for academic as well as socio-emotional support mainly because their social networks may be limited or non-existent shortly after their arrival to a new country. Needless to say faculty supervisors can have a profound effect on these non-native students (Adrian-Taylor, Noels, & Tischler, 2007). Unfortunately research shows faculty and international graduate students may experience greater dissatisfaction and conflict in their supervisor/supervisee relationships than native students, as did Luis and Campbell. Faculty need to be made aware that cultural relations in the student's home country may not reflect norms in other cultures when it comes to respect, interpersonal communication, delivering feedback, accepting responsibilities, and time interacting together. To resolve misunderstanding or conflict that arises with international students, Adrian-Taylor et al. recommended more open discussion, formulating a work contract, and offering useful, periodic supervisory feedback on the student's work and their overall progress.

Millett and MacKenzie (1995) studied minority students in assistantship roles. Non-minorities received more administrative assistantships that minority students, while minorities fared better at receiving teaching and research assistantships. In general, assistantships helped students integrate into their programs, interact with faculty, and participate in opportunities for greater socialization.

Egalitarian placement of diverse groups in various types of assistantships appeared critical to student success and program enhancement. Furthermore, Smeby (2000) learned that females prefer same gender pairings rather than cross-gender pairings in supervisor/supervisee relationships particularly in the natural sciences as compared to the softer sciences. Perhaps LaToya worked better with Campbell than Jefferies because of the gender pairing. These differences should be considered when matching supervisors with students for work assignments.

Faculty supervisors may not always be culturally trained to supervise members of another gender, race, and/or ethnicity. As such, ignoring or using supervisees' ethnicity may ultimately affect their professional identity development. Jefferies may have felt LaToya's placement in a high-profile office would be beneficial to both of them rather than thinking what would have been best for LaToya's professional development or a better skill match.

Furthermore, supervisors may gain reputations for cultural insensitivity or their inability to properly supervise minority or non-native students (Gardner, 2002). Faculty need to be more inclusive and sensitive and better versed in appropriate cross-cultural communication skills and be able to openly and honestly discuss issues of race and ethnicity with supervisees in order to form more effective learning environments (Subramanian et al, 2013). Frank discussions between supervisor/supervisee on cross-cultural issues, beliefs, and basic knowledge that leads to strong, positive interpersonal relationships is encouraged especially when done with "empathy, humility, genuineness, and respect" (Gardner, 2002, p. 103).

Faculty supervision of students should contribute to their socialization into the program, department, and profession. However, faculty must work with supervisees to ensure professional competence by providing them with opportunities for professional development. Researching Latino students in STEM fields, Lechuga (2011) suggested faculty develop a "concern for their students' psychological and emotional health, and overall well-being" (p. 763). Supervisors considered giving students more responsibility when minimal supervision proved important to their development. This may have caused the difficulty between Campbell and Luis. In fact, students need to "take direction well and work efficiently and independently" (p. 765) in order to gain the most out of the experience, which is not what Luis chose to do much to Campbell's surprise and dismay. It is also important for supervisors to "provide students the space to make mistakes" in order to "demonstrate self-sufficiency" (p. 766). As agents of socialization, "faculty serve as ambassadors of the profession by imbuing students with a sense of professional responsibility and introducing them into the culture of academe" (p. 768).

SUPERVISING GRADUATE ASSISTANTS

Still Scratching their Heads

At a regularly scheduled faculty meeting speaking on behalf of the rest of the faculty, Professor Wozniak asked the chair why the three department graduate assistants spent their time assigned to the administrative assistant completing mindless clerical tasks. Wozniak argued that the students would be better served by giving them research-related tasks that would better address their socialization into the profession. The administrative assistant defended her position that the work of the department cannot be accomplished without the students' help. Faculty chimed in to say how they would use the graduate students to further their research agendas and agreed to share the students' time. After a brief discussion, the chair sided with the administrative assistant.

Perna and Hudgins (1996) learned that some graduate assistants (GAs) saw their supervisors as their "boss." This clearly colored their professional relationship as opposed to the student viewing their supervisor as more of a guide or mentor. Wozniak's department sent mixed messages that clerical administrative duties took preference over professional student socialization especially considering that the faculty knew students would have benefited greatly from working with them on their research. *How* supervisors supervise students tends to be as significant as *what* they assign students to do. If having a graduate assistantship helps with professional socialization, then assigning students grunt work, monitoring their work unnecessarily, or setting unrealistic deadlines or demands seems counterproductive. GAs from this particular department left with little professional skill, shortchanging their experience. Instead, assistantships should give students greater entre into professionalism through working with faculty in more meaningful ways. Professionalism can be encouraged by supervisor assignments that challenge students to reach higher levels in their professional development (Bloom et al, 1984; Krathwohl et al, 1964; Nyquist et al, 1999).

SUPERVISING TEACHING ASSISTANTS

Students deserve consistency in their training if they are to become more effective instructors and academics. Teaching assistants (TAs) need uniform supervision rather than haphazard, inconsistent oversight (Bowen & Rudenstine, 1992). In addition, supervisors have a professional responsibility to provide timely, constructive, continual feedback to supervisees in order to improve student self-efficacy (Baltimore, 1998). Activities that contribute to self-efficacy include observations of teaching, pep talks from faculty supervisors, prior pedagogical training or classroom experience, delivering practice lectures to which faculty supervisors provide feedback, and altering student role demands commensurate with their current skill levels and experience (Prieto & Meyers, 1999). Faculty development offices can help graduate students new to teaching in labs and classrooms improve their instructional delivery techniques (Goodlad, 1997). Mid-semester evaluations/observations by supervisors and faculty development personnel would be as helpful as end of semester evaluations.

In their study of engineering TAs, Mena, Diefes-Dux, and Capabianco (2013) found that interaction varied such that some supervisees experienced semesters with minimal or unstructured supervision that was more informal than formal. Mena et al stressed the importance of greater faculty authenticity in regularly scheduled meetings and interactions with supervisees. Supervisors with multiple TAs might group them together to form a community of learners in order to facilitate greater interaction and increase peer support (Joys of (top-notch) supervision, 2005; Mena et al, 2013). Austin and McDaniels (2006) recommend guided reflection between supervisees and supervisors in order to allow students to ask supervisors questions so that each can reflect on their own teaching experiences. Ideally, the supervisor/supervisee relationship could be less formal and hierarchical and more seasoned colleague to future colleague.

81

SUPERVISING RESEARCH ASSISTANTS

Remember Howard?

When Professors Long, Short, and Talle arrived on campus as new assistant professors, they were pleased to hear that they would share a seasoned graduate assistant, Howard. Howard informed them he had been there six years so he looked and acted more like a tenured professor. Because these new faculty had work for Howard to do, they arranged to plan ahead for their needs so as not to overtax him. One day Howard came to Professor Long and said he was particularly busy this week working for the other professors. She understood. He also went to Professor Short and sobbed the same story and she understood. He approached Professor Talle and he understood, too. Then Howard disappeared for a few weeks. Apparently Howard assumed that Long, Short, and Talle never visited the water cooler at the same time. When they did, they asked the pivotal question: Anybody seen Howard?

Doctoral students working closely with a professor as research assistants (RAs) have different expectations than those working as teaching assistants. The roles are dissimilar and the status is different. RAs recognized especially how important conducting research was to their professor's academic life versus teaching (Golde, 1998). As a seasoned RA, Howard knew that quite well but apparently in the interim he also learned how to outwit three unsuspecting faculty members new to the department.

Differences exist between junior and senior faculty and how they approached RA supervision. Junior faculty often expect to develop their graduate assistants to do research but senior faculty in addition to this saw reasons to also develop students professionally and to network in the profession (Lechuga, 2011). New faculty may not always be well versed as to how much work time to expect from RAs or what all that work should entail. Departmental guidelines should offer some assistance. Long, Short, and Talle appeared to have worked out a schedule for Howard but perhaps they needed to consult other colleagues for clarity and especially the chair to report Howard's unprofessional behavior.

Supervisors need to be visible and interact with their graduate supervisees *frequently*. Likewise, supervisees must check in with their supervisors frequently and not disappear off the radar like Howard.

Research supervisors may wish to encourage their students, especially more advanced ones, to select and research their own problems in the lab rather than always dovetail with the supervisor. Faculty should model the supervisory role to RAs (and TAs and GAs as well) and help them understand the expectations of supervision (Joys of (top-notch) supervision, 2005).

SUPERVISING OFFSITE/IN THE FIELD

Aspland, Edwards, O'Leary, and Ryan (1999) argued consistency varied in faculty supervision in academic venues versus clinical venues. This may be linked to faculty and student interaction with additional "field relevant clinical faculty" and other professionals/practitioners (Guthrie & Marsh, 2009, p. 2). Expectations for professional doctorates mean supervisor, supervisee, and practitioner must interact. This requires faculty to share their supervisory duties with offsite practitioners and involve them in curricular areas and program design as well as in supervisee evaluations. Professional/executive programs offer doctoral students multiple advisors and possible mentors; however, academic faculty may not be versed in how to traverse this aspect of supervising. Site supervisors, in turn, may not always recognize their own role in relation to academic faculty or academic expectations for doctoral student interns (Guthrie & Marsh, 2009).

Communication between supervisor and supervisee (Bradner, Crossman, Vanderbilt, Gary, & Munson, 2013) and also between the faculty supervisor and the field/offsite supervisor should be early and ongoing. Guidelines should be communicated to supervisees at or prior to an orientation session (Sharkin & Coulter, 2009). Faculty and the offsite supervisor(s) must communicate what expectations faculty has for the site supervisor(s) with regard to the graduate student supervisee. Sharkin and Coulter viewed this as supervising the supervisor(s). They recommended writing a training agreement or contract to "clarify and ensure the mutual understanding of expectations and goals" (p. 164). Needless to say, all three parties must agree to the terms which should also include evaluation methods to be applied and times and types of communication to be used.

Agreements are essential because faculty looks for how the student will be applying classroom knowledge to the training situation while the site supervisor may be more concerned with the quality of services provided by the graduate student intern/clinician. Faculty also needs to be aware when offsite supervisors cross boundaries and rely too heavily on supervisees. Faculty and offsite supervisor(s) and the student should convene at least once per semester to assess student progress. If the student needs to switch offsite supervisor(s) or sites, that should be addressed openly and collaboratively and communicated promptly to the faculty supervisor (Sharkin & Coulter, 2009).

Students may not always be thoroughly screened before performing an internship, clinical, or preceptorship. Furthermore, field/offsite supervisors may not possess the necessary evaluation skills to recognize marginal students or the support from academic faculty if they needed to dismiss or fail a student in an internship or clinical (Luhanga et al, 2008). Handbook guidelines and policies clearly outlining and governing faculty/clinical/preceptor situations should exist along with frequent faculty communication with field supervisors monitoring student progress.

Because physicians utilize case methods daily to teach and to solve medical issues, the case approach to help train faculty advisors to supervise medical students' improvement of their skills seems logical. Faculty generates short case vignettes and shares them at periodic case conference meetings with faculty and offsite supervisors. It permits faculty to gain insight from colleagues in how to recognize problems and to resolve them using relevant literature and personal experiences to inform responses. This approach can be adapted to any discipline or professional area (Shocket, Cayea, Levine, & Wright, 2010).

TEAM SUPERVISION

Ray and Altekruse (2000) advocated increasing supervisory strategies using group/team methods and decreasing student isolation in order to improve skill development and ensure personal and professional development. This can be enhanced with prompt feedback from the supervisor especially in practicum and internship situations and to further enhance skill development.

Team supervision provides social and intellectual benefits beyond one-to-one supervision. The team approach benefits junior faculty learning the basics of the advisor/supervisor roles as Professors Long, Short and Talle illustrated. It highlights the more subtle political nuances associated with advising and supervising with these professors learning on the job. Team supervision can be one means for faculty to model compromise to students following faculty disagreement over teaching or research issues. Team approaches increase feedback opportunities and provide colleagues with an opportunity to demonstrate and model collegiality (Manathunga, 2012). Team supervision approaches challenge the traditional master/apprentice model so in order for students and faculty to benefit, faculty must incorporate new approaches to their supervising skill set.

ETHICS OF SUPERVISION

Faculty advisors and supervisors share responsibility for providing students with codes of ethics and instill in them ethical obligations with regard to teaching, research, and professional practice (Artino & Brown, 2009). Supervisors should model research and publication ethics to supervisees so these can be inculcated. They have a tacit need to maintain academic integrity and uphold normative ethical standards of research in the profession (Gray & Jordan, 2012). Expectations for student and faculty behavior in academic settings are no more or less important than behavioral expectations in the lab, clinical, internship, or practicum setting (Cole & Lewis, 1993). Universities and professional associations must formulate policy on academic integrity and compile, practice, and communicate a code of conduct (East & Donnelly, 2012). Turner and Beemsterboer (2003) emphasized the role of faculty in addressing these ethical codes, discussing their significance with students, monitoring situations, and subsequently, enforcing violations of stated codes.

What Tangled Webs We Weave

Professor Brylinsky established a contract business compiling institutional fact books for numerous small, faith-based, liberal arts colleges. Brylinsky hired two graduate assistants to help him. He told Margie and Tony privately that their life would be better if they each maintained a "close relationship" with him. Professor Brylinsky, Margie, Tony, and a few other invited senior faculty, Professors Ho, Morgenstern, and Spaniel agreed to present a weekend institutional research workshop at one of the contracted faith-based colleges. Early in the workshop, Ho and Spaniel realized little if any organization or preparation went into this workshop. This jeopardized their program and university reputation. Brylinsky began sessions late and presented the material haphazardly. The audience sensed it also. To ease the tension, Brylinsky decided to have a party Saturday evening and serve alcohol. Ho and Spaniel declined to attend but Brylinsky insisted that Margie, Tony, and Morgenstern stay. The following morning when it was time to pack the van and head back home, Brylinsky failed to appear. Morgenstern apologized saying Brylinsky had too much to drink and he was too ill to travel. Everyone should go on without him. Back home, Margie's and Tony's advisors encouraged them to resign their assistantship as soon as possible. When Tony's final pay check never came, he told his advisor. Brylinsky eventually paid Tony with a personal check which Tony thought about reporting to Contracts and Grants but never did.

Mieczkowski (1995) argued that the administration knows that certain faculty supervises graduate students poorly and yet they do nothing. What is worse, he admonished, as bureaucrats they tend to find plausible excuses for it and disregard or dismiss further complaints which insulate and legitimize such behavior, if not passively justify it. Note that everyone knew what was going on yet excuses for Brylinsky's behavior were accepted, academic administration as well as Contracts and Grants were not informed subsequently of his breaches of ethics and propriety.

While this approach to supervision can raise ethical issues or role conflicts between supervisors and supervisees, it challenges each party to function in new roles that move them to a more unequal status. As such, honest critique or challenges may not be received well, hence Tony's reluctance to follow up with Contracts and Grants. Departments/schools/universities must provide uniform guidelines and procedures to faculty supervisors and students. Supervisors may also need to set more specific ground rules for their own assistants, interns, or trainees (Kirton, Straker, Brown, Jack, & Jenks, 2011). Faculty needs to monitor serious deviations from those guidelines and policies rather than turn a blind eye or deaf ear as did the professors in this instance.

While inculcating disciplinary/professional practice in students, supervisory teams can be more effective than a solitary supervisor. They can watch "each other . . . causing each other to display particular supervisory technologies of self" (Manathunga, 2012, p. 32). In other words, each team member may be particularly adept at different aspects of the supervisory role thus complementing the other faculty on the team. Team members can temper the critical responses of other colleagues as well as clarify them, serving to reduce student confusion. The supervisory team approach allows for ethical checks of one another but only if Professors Ho, Morgenstern, and Spaniel and Tony's and Margie's advisors are willing to come forward.

Manathunga (2012) posited that "team supervision causes an increase in supervisory self-regulation as supervisors monitor their own words and actions more carefully . . . than they might do in private meetings with their students" (p. 36). Margie and Tony would have benefited from this approach. Each did the right thing and told their advisors who issued appropriate advice to their advisees. Perhaps they even confided in each other before contacting their advisors. The missing link was the passive response of the senior faculty who knew of Brylinsky's ethical breaches and did nothing to correct them.

SUPERVISION AND GRADUATE STUDENT UNIONIZATION

Teaching and research assistants hold ambiguous status in the campus hierarchy because they are half-time students and half-time instructors (Parsons & Platt, 1973). Administrators use TAs to cover classes more so than concentrate on using assistantship opportunities to help prepare students for future professional roles (Austin & McDaniels, 2006). In fact, students presumed an assistantship would ensure them greater integration, collaboration, and less isolation in their programs (Ellis, 2001). Students complained that little TA/GA/RA training and minimal opportunities for faculty/student collaborative research opportunities were made available to them. Students contended that the supervisor/advisor role and the apprentice/future colleague role implies some measure of sharing and collaborating rather than a purely perpetual follower to leader situation (Buraway, 2005; Sharnoff, 1993). Often the relationship gets muddied as faculty and students adapt their roles to new situations.

Julius and Gumport (2002) explored why graduate students chose to unionize and how unionization might affect aspects of the supervisor/supervisee relationship. Historically unionization emerged in response to university expansion, fiscal belt-tightening, and possible graduate assistant exploitation as an inexpensive labor source in courses faculty no longer wanted to teach. The prevailing sentiment among graduate students, however, was that "unionization [is] a viable means to address power imbalances between themselves, the institution, and the faculty"

(Julius & Gumport, 2002, p. 198). While attempts to organize in unions date back to the 1960s and 1970s, graduate student unionization garnered substantial inroads nearer the end of the 20th century and the beginning of the 21st.

Rogers, Eaton, and Voos (2013) found that student membership in a union has not had negative repercussions but, on the contrary, offers a means to delineate the supervisor/supervisee relationship and clarify supervisor obligations to the student. Misinterpretation of labor union agreements could have the potential to disrupt supervisor/supervisee relationships but significant issues have not yet been reported. Because some graduate students may be naïve about unions, not particularly savvy to union negotiation procedures, or even cognizant from where their paycheck emanates (hard money, soft money, grant money), unions may serve to prevent supervisee exploitation. Unions may especially protect graduate assistants on soft money who misinterpret key supervisor signals and hold out hope for continued renewal that might never come, thereby missing opportunities for sponsorship elsewhere (Perna & Hudgins, 1996).

EVALUATING FACULTY SUPERVISORS

While graduate students evaluate faculty teaching, rarely are they given an opportunity to formally rate faculty supervision of their assistantship, internship, or clinical. Although Marsh, Rowe, and Martin (2002) found that students evaluated their advisor similarly across disciplines, the results of the evaluation might be helpful only to that professor. Aggregate sample data may offer little information of value to a program or department.

Marsh et al (2002) also recognized that despite similarities in a supervisor's performance over time, there is no formal standard level of acceptable supervisory performance; therefore, no comparative standard against which to judge faculty performance exists. In fact, Manathunga and Goozee (2007) envisioned super-vision on a multiple continuum moving from hands-on advising to laissez-faire advising for faculty and moving from dependent to autonomous on the part of students. In their study, students regarded themselves as more autonomous and faculty labeled their own personal style as more hands-off. Supervisor/supervisee self-reports may provide some information but evaluation needs to be cross-checked in order to provide more helpful information.

BEST PRACTICES

- Formulate, distribute, and practice ethical codes of behavior (White & Nonnamaker, 2011). Departments, schools, and professional associations should utilize these frequently at professional development sessions.
- Formal and informal periodic evaluations and self-reports of faculty supervision (White & Nonnamaker, 2011; Manthunga & Goozee, 2007) done in conjunction

with annual performance appraisals or as part of a professional development experience should be considered.

■ In addition to direct supervision, supervisors should encourage students to watch "video tapes of their own practice teaching," encourage "role playing teaching activities," and provide constructive feedback (Prieto & Scheel, 2008, p. 54).

■ Connect supervisory assignments to each student's area of study to maximize their teaching, research, and professionalization (Weidman, Twale, & Stein, 2001; White & Nonnamaker, 2011).

■ Acknowledge differences in gender, race, and international status when making supervisor/supervisee assignments. Consider team/group supervisory strategies both on campus and with offsite/field practitioners.

RESOURCES

■ Departments or schools looking to formulate an instrument to evaluate ethical practice in supervisor/supervisee relationships will find a good example of one appended in Gray and Jordan (2012).

■ Visit La Trobe University's website at www.latrobe.edu.au/students/learning/academic-integrity/academic-integrity-module for an academic integrity module and read more about it in East and Donnelly (2012) (retrieved June 21, 2014).

■ Faculty desiring conflict management training should contact their campus human resources department for direction.

■ Offices of international students may help faculty learn more about diverse cultures and how to relate in a supervisory capacity to non-native students.

REFERENCES

Adrian-Taylor, S., Noels, K., & Tischler, K. (2007). Conflict between international graduate students and faculty supervisors: Toward effective conflict prevention and management strategies. *Journal of Studies in International Education*, *11*(1), 90–117.

Artino, A., & Brown, S. (2009). Ethics in educational research: A comparative analysis of graduate student and faculty beliefs. *College Student Journal*, *43*, 599–615.

Aspland, T., Edwards, H., O' Leary, J., & Ryan, Y. (1999). Tracking new direction in the evaluation of postgraduate supervision. *Innovative Higher Education*, *24*, 127–147.

Austin, A., & McDaniels, M. (2006). Preparing the professoriat of the future: Graduate student socialization for faculty roles. In J. Smart (Ed.), *Higher education handbook of theory and research*, Volume 21 (pp. 397–456). Dordrecht, Netherlands: Springer.

Baltimore, M. (1998). Supervision ethics: Counseling the supervisor. *The Family Journal of Counseling and Therapy for Couples and Families*, *6*, 312–325.

Biaggio, M., Paget, T., & Chenoweth, M. (1997). A model for ethical management of faculty–student dual relationships. *Professional Psychology: Research and Practice*, *28*, 184–189.

Bloom, B., Engehart, M., Furst, F., Hill, W., & Krathwohl, D. (Eds.) (1984). *Taxonomy of educational objectives. Book 1: Cognitive domain*. New York: Longman.

Border, C., & Barba, W. (1998, November). *Graduate student support and the graduate education experience*. Paper presented at the annual meeting of the Association for the Study of Higher Education, Miami, FL. (ERIC Document Reproduction Service No. ED427 577)

Bowen, H., & Rudenstine, N. (1992). *In pursuit of the PhD*. Princeton, NJ: Princeton University Press.

Bradner, M., Crossman, S., Vanderbilt, A., Gary, J., & Munson, P. (2013). Career advising in family medicine: A theoretical framework for structuring the medical student–faculty advising interview. *Medical Education Online, 18*, 21173.

Braxton, J., Proper, E., & Bayer, A. (2011). *Professors behaving badly*. Baltimore: Johns Hopkins University Press.

Brubaker, J., & Rudy, W. (1997). *Higher education in transition* (4th ed.). New Brunswick, NJ: Transaction Publishers.

Buerkel-Rothfus, N., & Gray, P. (1990) Graduate teaching assistants in speech communication and non-communication departments: A national survey. *Communication Education, 39*, 292–307.

Buraway, M. (2005). Combat in the dissertation zone. *American Sociologist, 36*(2), 42–56.

Chiang, S. (2009). Personal power and positional power in a power-full "I": A discourse analysis of doctoral dissertation supervision. *Discourse and Communication, 3*, 255–272.

Cole, B., & Lewis, R. (1993). Gatekeeping through termination of unsuitable social work students: Legal issues and guidelines. *Journal of Social Work Education, 29*, 150–159.

East, J., & Donnelly, J. (2012). Taking responsibility for academic integrity: A collaborative teaching and learning design. *Journal of University Teaching and Learning Practice, 9*(3), article 2.

Ellis, E. (2001). The impact of race and gender on graduate school socialization, satisfaction with doctoral study, and commitment to degree completion. *The Western Journal of Black Studies, 25*, 30–45.

Gardner, R. (2002). Cross cultural perspectives in supervision. *The Western Journal of Black Studies, 26*, 98–106.

Geiger, R. (2007). Research, graduate education, and the ecology of American universities: An interpretive history. In H. Wechsler, L. Goodchild, & L. Eisenmann (Eds.), *The history of higher of education* (3rd ed.), (pp. 316–331). ASHE Reader series. Boston: Pearson Custom Publishing.

Golde, C. (1998). Beginning graduate school: Explaining first year doctoral attrition. In M. Anderson (Ed.), *The experience of being in graduate school: An exploration* (pp. 55–64). New Directions for Higher Education no. 101. Amherst, NY: Prometheus Books.

Goodlad, S. (1997). Responding to the perceived needs of graduate teaching assistants. *Studies in Higher Education, 22*, 83–92.

Goodyear, R., Crego, C., & Johnston, M. (1992). Ethical issues in the supervision of student researchers. *Professional Psychology: Research and Practice, 23*, 203–210.

Gottlieb, M., Robinson, K., & Younggren, J. (2007). Multiple relations in supervision: Guidance for administrators, supervisors, and students. *Professional Psychology: Research and Practice, 38*, 241–247.

Granello, D. (2000). Encouraging the cognitive development of supervisors: Using Bloom's taxonomy in supervision. *Counselor Education and Supervision, 40*, 31–46.

Gray, P., & Jordan, S. (2012). Supervisors and academic integrity: Supervisors as exemplars and mentors. *Journal of Academic Ethics, 10*, 299–311.

Guthrie, J., & Marsh, D. (2009). Introduction to the special issue on the educational doctorate. *Peabody Journal of Education, 84*, 1–2.

Jenks, C., & Riesman, D. (1977). *The American revolution.* Chicago: University of Chicago Press.

Joys of (top-notch) supervision. (2005). *Nature, 434*(7032), 421.

Julius D., & Gumport, P. (2002). Graduate student unionization: Catalysts and consequences. *Review of Higher Education, 26*, 187–216.

Kirton, J., Straker, K., Brown, J., Jack, B., & Jenks, A. (2011). A marriage of convenience? A qualitative study of colleague supervision of master's level dissertations. *Nurse Education Today, 31*, 861–865.

Krathwohl, D., Bloom, B., & Masia, B. (1964). *Taxonomy of educational objectives. Book 2: Affective domain.* New York: Longman.

Lechuga, V. (2011). Faculty–graduate student mentoring relationships: Mentors' perceived roles and responsibilities. *Higher Education, 62*, 757–771.

Luhanga, F., Yonge, O., & Myrick, F. (2008). Precepting an unsafe student: The role of the faculty. *Nurse Educator Today, 28*, 227–231.

Madsen, C. (2003). Instruction and supervision of graduate students in music education. *Research Studies in Education, 21*, 72–79.

Manathunga, C. (2012). Supervisors watching supervisors. *Australian Universities' Review, 54*(1), 29–37.

Manathunga, C., & Goozee, J. (2007). Challenging the dual assumption of the "Always/Already" autonomous student and effective supervisor. *Teaching in Higher Education, 12*, 309–322.

Marsh, H., Rowe, K., & Martin, A. (2002). PhD students' evaluation of research supervision. *Journal of Higher Education, 73*, 313–348.

Mena, I., Diefes-Dux, H., & Capabianco, B. (2013). Socialization experiences resulting from doctoral engineering teaching assistantships. *Journal of Higher Education, 84*, 189–212.

Mieczkowski, B. (1995). *The rot at the top: Dysfunctional bureaucracy in academe.* Lanham, MD: University Press of America.

Millett, C., & MacKenzie, S. (1995, November). *An exploratory study of the role of financial aid in minority doctoral education*. Paper presented at the annual meeting of the Association for the Study of Higher Education, Orlando, FL. (ERIC Document Reproduction Service No. ED391 411)

Nyquist, J., Manning, L., Wulff, D., Austin, A., Sprague, J., Fraser, P., Calcagno, C., & Woodard, B. (1999). On the road to becoming a professor: The graduate student experience. *Change, 31*(3), 18–27.

Parsons, T., & Platt, G. (1973). *The American university*. Cambridge, MA: Harvard University Press.

Perna, L., & Hudgins, C. (1996, November). *The graduate assistantship: Facilitator of graduate students' professional socialization*. Paper presented at the annual meeting of the Association for the Study of Higher Education, Memphis, TN. (ERIC Document Reproduction Service No. ED402 822)

Prieto, L., & Meyers, S. (1999). Effects of training and supervision on the self-efficacy of psychology graduate teaching assistants. *Teaching of Psychology, 26*, 264–266.

Prieto, L., & Scheel, K. (2008). Teaching assistantship training in counseling psychology. *Counseling Psychology Quarterly, 21*, 49–59.

Ray, D., & Altekruse, M. (2000). Effectiveness of group supervision versus combined group and individual supervision. *Counselor Education and Supervision, 40*, 19–30.

Rogers, S., Eaton, A., & Voos, P. (2013). Effects of unionization on graduate student employees: Faculty–student relations, academic freedom, and pay. *Industry and Labor Relations, 66*, 487–510.

Scarborough, J., Bernard, J., & Morse, R. (2006). Boundary considerations between doctoral and master's students. *Counseling and Values, 51*, 53–65.

Sharkin, B., & Coulter, L. (2009). Communication between college counselors and academic faculty when supervising graduate student trainees. *Journal of College Counseling, 12*, 162–169.

Sharnoff, E. (1993, December). *Neither fish nor fowl: Graduate students, unionization, and the academy*. Paper presented at the annual meeting of the Modern Language Association, Toronto. (ERIC Document Reproduction Service No. ED375 743)

Shocket, R., Cayea, D., Levine, R., & Wright, S. (2010). Using medical student case presentations to help faculty learn to be better advisors. *Academic Medicine, 84*, 578–579.

Smeby, J. (2000). Same-gender relationships in graduate supervision. *Higher Education, 40*, 53–67.

Subramanian, J., Anderson, V., Morgaine, K., & Thompson, W. (2013). Effective and ineffective supervision in postgraduate dental education: A qualitative study. *European Journal of Dental Education, 17*(1), e142–e150.

Syverson, P. (1982). *1981 doctorate recipients from United States universities. Summary report*. Washington, DC: National Academy of Sciences—National Research Council, Commission on Human Resources. (ERIC Document Preproduction Service No. ED221 134)

Turner, S., & Beemsterboer, P. (2003). Enhancing academic integrity: Formulating effective honor codes. *Journal of Dental Education*, *67*, 1122–1129.

Walker, G., Golde, C., Jones, L., Bueschel, A., & Hutchings, P. (2008). *The formation of scholars*. San Francisco: Jossey-Bass.

Weidman, J., Twale, D., & Stein, E. (2001). *Socialization of graduate and professional students in higher education: A perilous passage?* San Francisco: Jossey-Bass.

White, J., & Nonnamaker, J. (2011). Supervising graduate students. In Roper, L. (Ed.), *Supporting and supervising mid-level professionals* (pp. 43–54). New Directions for Student Services no. 136. Hoboken, NJ: Wiley Periodicals.

Wong, H., & Sanders, J. (1983). Gender differences in the attainment of doctorates. *Sociological Perspectives*, *26*, 29–49.

Woods, S., Burgess, L., Kaminetzky, C., McNeill, D., Pinheiro, S., & Heflin, M. (2010). Defining the role of advisors and mentors in post graduate medical education: Faculty perceptions, roles, responsibilities, and resource needs. *Journal of Graduate Medical Education*, *2*, 195–200.

Chapter 7

Conquering the Academic Wild West

Advising Virtually Using Social Media

The invention of the printing press, the electric typewriter, and the computer once revolutionized the faculty workload. Faculty connected with students by phone or in person and ideally they touched base sometime during the semester. Programs offered on-campus orientation sessions to welcome new cohorts of students. Assigned advisors met with advisees to outline a plan of study. Faculty handed students a copy of the graduate student handbook. Peers provide peers with additional information ranging from probably not true to totally false. This "corridor gossip" panics students, making them question if they have the wrong advisor. But, advisors may not be able to schedule a meeting for weeks. Those were the days!

Today, students and faculty can communicate face to face but not in person through Skype; receive accurate, consistent reminders through Twitter; connect professionally with fellow students on LinkedIn; and/or connect socially with peers on Facebook. The future is here but like any new territory it must be conquered by its inhabitants. Uses of social media and online communication in graduate faculty advising may parallel the tales of the Wild West but further research may be needed to learn how to tame it (McEachern, 2011).

Tay and Allen (2011) suggested that today's student constructs knowledge differently than did previous generations. Students expect faculty immediacy and presence either through social, physical, or virtual means (Poellhuber, Roy, & Anderson, 2011). Incorporating online communication and social media into the advisor/advisee relationship makes perfect sense. While these approaches will serve as a learning experience for faculty and students, Tay and Allen concluded that *how* faculty designs their communication using these social media options will prove to be far more significant than is the technology being used. Horizontal student communication with peers poses fewer challenges for students who wish to interact through social media with or without faculty input. Using digital communication to facilitate group vertical and horizontal communication may require some basic training for faculty (Charsky, Kish, Briskin, Hathaway, Walsh, & Barajas, 2009).

To Be Or Not To Be ... Online

Professor Van Slyke secured a faculty position at a for-profit institution whose courses were all delivered online. He enjoyed face-to-face teaching and interacting with students at his previous traditional institution. Van Slyke had taught a few online courses before through the local community college but never advised students online, a new job requirement. How difficult could it be, he thought. About midway through the semester, the division chair contacted Van Slyke to discuss several complaints she had received from students. Apparently, these students asked for an advisor change because Van Slyke's email communications were "confusing and infrequent and seldom returned in a timely fashion." The students contemplated dropping out of the program unless they were assigned an advisor who was more responsive and sensitive to their concerns. Van Slyke explained to his chair that because he was new to the program, advising posed its own set of challenges.

Online learning is self-directive, interactive, and ongoing. Advising students online should follow the same pattern as online learning: The advisor and advisee(s) communicate with each other regularly, and share the same issues they would have shared if they met in the advisors' on-campus office (Draves, 2002). However, teaching and/or advising online may not suit the desires or abilities of every faculty member (Bocchi, Eastman, & Swift, 2004). Advising and supervising online implies the familiarity and willingness to use multiple electronic/virtual communication modes effectively. Advisors need to create virtual communities of advisees through the use of proper communication techniques, be available to students, and flexible with their schedules.

Faculty is encouraged to receive training and perfect virtual communication skills before going online. Luke and Gordon (2011) cautioned advisors/supervisors to "be intentional about their language use and closely monitor the ways in which the form and function affect the supervising alliance" (p. 287) with their advisee/supervisees. Furthermore, having students "reflect on how they affect and are affected by the supervisory discourse" should be done regularly (p. 287). Like Professor Van Slyke, faculty not totally committed to online programming should be cautioned about advising graduate students online, and when committed should seek professional development beforehand.

IMMEDIACY IN ONLINE ADVISING AND SUPERVISING

Communication between advisors and advisees affects their mutual relationship and determines if it leads to positive or negative outcomes. Immediacy in communication encompasses verbal and non-verbal elements which include eye contact, facial expressions, personal space, feedback, and praise. Positive immediacy behaviors emerge through advisor/advisee closeness, interaction patterns, and potential bonding (Mehrabian, 1971).

Faculty advisors need to be aware of the verbal and non-verbal messages they send to their advisees. Faculty advising in distance learning programs must maintain an added burden of continued communication with advisees to decrease the likelihood that the advisee will misinterpret aspects associated with non-verbal immediacy. Wrench and Punyanunt (2004) found that immediacy and visibility in asynchronous online learning can be limited, therefore creating isolation between advisor, advisee, and peers.

Most essential for advisors/supervisors working online is "to create a positive work relationship" that leads to "mutual understanding" because virtual communication cannot recreate non-verbal face-to-face visual clues (Scarcia-King, 2011, p. 58). Online messages should be just as encouraging to the student as those delivered face to face.

Janes (2006) learned that students desired faculty "presence" online which substituted for the lack of face-to-face interpersonal connections. Students also sought an emotional connection with faculty as well and believed their advisors/supervisors were effective when they demonstrated that they cared about them. When writing or reading virtual communication, advisors and advisees must interpret the emotional tone sent in the message that is more easily discerned in face-to-face communication.

Advisors/supervisors must "recognize and understand the impact of emotions on communication and relationships" when connecting virtually so that "the technology does not impede the intuition, judgment, and interpersonal connection required to be engaged, supportive, and responsive" (Scarcia-King, 2011, pp. 65–66). Kim, Liu, and Bonk (2005) agreed that the emotional connection and feedback immediacy can clarify tone by incorporating frequent advisee telephone contact with electronic modes of communication. Messages will need to be more intentional and carefully constructed and proofread to ensure the message's tone comes across as intended.

Attempting to create immediacy online can be accomplished in several ways. The addition of YouTube videos and/or voiceover PowerPoint slides located in course management systems or attached to a faculty webpage accessible to all students creates a more personal environment for students where they can see and hear their faculty advisor as a live, human entity (McEachern, 2011). To further ensure clarity, Scarcia-King (2011) recommended the use of visual aids to assist advisees such as screen shots, voiceover PowerPoints, web links, or other email attachments like cognitive maps or flow charts. These visual aids can illustrate time lines or program specifics. Web conferencing on Skype can assist with increasing verbal and non-verbal aspects of advisor immediacy.

What faculty communicates to students regarding their personal style, level of approachability, personality, and degree of engagement can be first expressed through online or blended coursework. Faculty can give positive clues regarding their advising style to students and increase their advisees' comfort level when interacting with them virtually.

Faculty must create a culture that supports meaningful advising/supervision electronically. This requires quality institutional services and support as well as faculty commitment to online delivery and engagement in advising. Levels of advisor engagement when discerned by the advisee will affect subsequent positive or negative advisee/advisor involvement and interaction.

VARIETY AND CONSISTENCY IN ONLINE ADVISING AND SUPERVISING

From Traditional to Online

When the dean informed Professors McVay, Prathanawany, and Ervin that their traditionally delivered graduate program would have to be transitioned completely to an asynchronous online format, they diligently worked as a team to develop a quality curriculum even though they had no idea what to expect. Of paramount importance was recreating a community of learners that had distinguished their traditional face-to-face program. After implementation two years later, new challenges emerged for these professors. Ervin missed interacting with her advisees face to face, so she telephoned and scheduled off-campus lunches with them rather than communicate electronically. Difficulties with language and new technology posed problems for Prathanawany as he struggled to convey information to his advisees. McVay loved teaching online and sought various electronic mediums to interact continually with her advisees. The students realized that instead of a unified advising plan upon which they could all rely, three different advising approaches emerged that resulted in anxiety among this small graduate cohort, splintering their once prized learning community.

Beitz (1987) indicated that advising confined to on-campus visits in faculty offices and through telephone conversations limits advisor/advisee and supervisor/supervisee interaction. Fornshell (1993) noted that faculty advising could be incorporated into online classroom formats. Curry, Baldwin, and Sharpe (1998) reported that students preferred real-time telephone conversations as the primary method to communicate with faculty advisors followed by office visits and regular mail. Group advising at new student orientations occurred face to face. Despite more sophisticated communication methods, faculty and students reverted back to older options like Professor Ervin. However, a very small portion of the faculty respondents reported using video conferencing, videotapes, and computer chat (Curry et al, 1998). Times have changed and media have changed but human adaptation and incorporation of these changes lags behind as Professor Ervin and

Prathanawany learned firsthand. They created an online program but, unlike McVay, failed to incorporate the benefits of online learning into online advising. Media can help create learning communities rather than disband them but it takes professional development and a concerted effort on the part of faculty to adapt.

Charsky et al (2009) illustrated that using digital communication for academic purposes tends not to be universally embraced. The authors believed that students may possess more technical skill than faculty advisors, thus explaining why faculty has yet to initiate them. While digital options can draw faculty and students together, obviously advisors will be drawn out of their comfort zone even though social media may facilitate good advising in contemporary ways. Frequent usage and increased user comfort coupled with advances in technology may open doors to new applications or ways of adapting existing ones to the advising function (Hung & Yuen, 2010; Li, 2012; Tay & Allen, 2011).

ADVISING/SUPERVISING THROUGH SOCIAL MEDIA AND ELECTRONIC COMMUNICATION

Luna and Medina (2007) stated that previous graduate faculty advising revolved around staying connected with students and facilitating their program completion through telephone, voicemail, email, and face-to-face meetings. Luna and Medina suggested that chat rooms and electronic posting of pertinent resource information on faculty webpages could help assist advisees with advising concerns.

Richardson, MacRae, Schwartz, Bankston, and Kosten (2008) found that students desire immediate feedback; however, asynchronous online formats tended to harbor slow response times from faculty. As a result, students preferred real-time alternatives through phone conversations or in-person meetings. They expressed concerns regarding instructor availability and the need for other optional communication modes to satisfy concerns of an urgent nature.

The thought of 24/7 advising availability provides a chilling reason for faculty and administrations to develop strategic responses. Therefore, academe continues to explore the uses and adaptations for social media as Professor McVay illustrates. Exploring these adaptations in advising/supervising seems natural given the frequency with which many incoming graduate students already use social media (Li, 2012; Tay & Allen, 2011). Because incoming students spend their time in various digital communication activities such as connecting with friends and extended family, academic advising might likewise be enhanced. In fact, vertical communication between advisor/supervisor and advisee/supervisee can be expanded to include horizontal communication between all students of a particular advisor (Charsky et al, 2009).

Social media use overlaps theoretical and contextual perspectives of social learning (Lave & Wenger, 1991), social networks (Granovetter, 1973), and immediacy (Mehrabian, 1971). Social media encourages faculty to glance into the

97

graduate student world as a participant and voyeur, of sorts, rather than just enter it physically. Social media affords advisors/supervisors an opportunity to gain information and insight into the graduate student culture (Hung & Yuen, 2010; Li, 2012).

According to Granovetter (1973), the strength of a social tie must be a linear combination of time spent together, the degree of emotional intensity, reciprocity, and feeling within the mutual connection. Strong ties form strong networks that lead to the formation of a community or perceived sense of community. Sacks and Graves (2012) advocated that these networks be small enough to manage but large enough to accommodate students' needs for practical, high-quality information and advising. Faculty advisors can construct communities that distinguish master's from doctoral advisees or first-year doctoral students from the ABDs in their communications (Domizi, 2013).

Social media offers continuity. Electronically, students share thoughts, feelings, and concerns outside of their face-to-face meetings with faculty and peers. Social media offers advisors/supervisors and advisees/supervisees the opportunity to share information anywhere, anytime through options like Twitter, Facebook, and LinkedIn.

LINKING SOCIAL MEDIA AND ELECTRONIC COMMUNICATION TO RETENTION

New technologies can fill in the gaps between formal, structured advising meetings and ensure that all advisees obtain the same information updates (Lindbeck & Fodrey, 2010). Students in Li's (2012) study, communicating with their advisor through social media, established an informal cohort and support system. Junco, Heibergert, and Loken (2011) linked social media with student engagement by using Twitter for continuing discussions beyond class time; connecting with one another outside of class; coordinating and organizing group activities; providing handy reminders and updates; offering support; and fielding questions. Incorporating Twitter forged interpersonal relations, facilitated collaboration, strengthened connections, and encouraged informal advising. In addition, comfort and ease of interaction and candor increased as did additional opportunities to interact. The connections formed resulted in a sense of belonging and continual access to the exchange of vital information which lessened student disengagement (Junco et al, 2011).

Not everyone feels the same about electronic communication modes. Taylor, Jowi, Schreier, and Bertelsen (2004) found that African-American students more so than white students preferred face-to-face meetings with advisors over electronic means. White and black females preferred email communication but for only *some* aspects of advising. Poellhuber et al (2011) discovered that although men possess greater confidence in their technical ability and teamwork, women enjoy the social aspects of networking. Older students more so than their younger counterparts appeared interested in the collaboration afforded through social networking.

Using social media for diffusion of advising information is especially powerful when the medium is effectively matched with the stated purpose and the community being served (Camacho & Guilana, 2011). Faculty advisors should tailor advising strategies to meet the needs of unique populations of students. LinkedIn or Facebook can display important, relevant advising information. Twitter can respond to student questions quickly and also support microblogging. Emails allow for lengthier messages. YouTube videos linked to the advisor's personal webpage or course management system can explain graduate school or department procedures and introduce new program changes. Multiple mediums can be utilized instead of just one medium to convey everything (Melton & Hicks, 2011).

Tweets for the Tweet

Trying to oversee five interns per semester created issues for a prolific researcher. Professor Blyden decided to employ Twitter, web conferencing, and email to keep tabs on her interns. Instead of them focusing on their own plight, she wanted them to focus on how they were serving the needs of their clients and how they could share what they discovered in their case loads with each other under her supervision. Social media and electronic communication would keep them informed and up to date but it would also allow them to weigh in on each other's difficult cases without actually being there. Each intern had a smart phone and could without violating the privacy act share their concerns, issues, and triumphs with peers/colleagues rather than remain in a self- or university-imposed silo. Linking the off-site supervisor, Dr. Parillo, with Blyden and the interns proved helpful too, as together they embraced the media's potential for enhanced learning. Instead of waiting a week or two to meet with each other, individuals could work as a team in real time and resolve issues more authentically than they could without the social media and electronic connection.

Creating communities of learners through online advising teams can be vital to online programming and student success (Kim et al, 2005). Bazzoni (2000) raised the possibility of the student, faculty advisor, and internship supervisor triad working together as a social network using online and social media to communicate more frequently. Professor Blyden realized that her supervision, her students, the clients, and the supervising practitioner would each benefit in myriad ways from incorporating social media into the internship experience.

Because of the limited number of face-to-face advisors, volunteer emergency room faculty advisors in a similar situation paired with emergency medicine students who sought advisors not located on their premises. Internet usage was required not only for matching the pairs but also for facilitating their subsequent advising (Coates et al, 2004). Some fields, such as medicine, remain cautious but optimistic about the acceptance of social media into advising and internships (Jain & Maxson, 2011). Currently, social media in advising should employ options that suit individual advisor/advisee, supervisor/supervisee, and situational needs. However, the evaluation of these approaches based on their uses remains anecdotal and rogue until research further explores their benefits and challenges in diverse fields and situations (McEachern, 2011).

ONLINE ADVISING AND FACULTY/ADMINISTRATIVE CONCERNS

Metzger, Finley, Unbrich, and McAuley (2010) questioned the professional aspects of social media and digital communication as posing conflicts between the traditional role of advisee and advisor. Social media use for classroom purposes as well as advising purposes departs from social media use as a purely social entity. Therefore, care and caution are urged on the part of advisors/supervisors to maintain propriety through appropriate use of all media. Usage must convey professionalism and subsequently encourage advisors/supervisors and advisees/supervisees to adhere to ethical standards and codes of conduct in what and how they communicate (McEachern, 2011). Limiting what types of communication are to be dispersed electronically ultimately filters out more personal and non-programmatic and non-professional information unsuitable for public consumption (Camacho & Guilana, 2011; Richardson et al, 2008). Traditional or online institutions must preserve a social media culture of integrity (Lanier, 2006).

Advisors need not come across as unresponsive, detached, unsupportive, or aloof. To be effective online, advisors must outline expectations for communication and performance in a personal communication plan that explains communication modes and the frequency for sending, checking, and responding to advisee messages. More importantly, advisors must practice netiquette and expect netiquette from advisees to facilitate friendly, upbeat, and respectful interaction (Scarcia-King, 2011).

Guidelines for initiating advisor/advisee communication should be distributed online to students (Richardson et al, 2008). Those guidelines may come from faculty, department, college, graduate school, and/or university (Smailes & Gannon-Leary, 2011). Similarly, information about e-advising should be compiled in a short faculty online handbook (Curry et al, 1998) that emanates from the provost's or graduate dean's office and can be easily accessed on the campus website. Faculty senates may wish to weigh in on proposed content of both handbooks. Helpful resources and services should be linked to include course management systems, blogging, microblogging, and web-conferencing options supported by the university.

As a cautionary note, using social media requires changes in mindset on the part of advisors/supervisors who may not wish to conform to consumer approaches in order to meet student needs (Junco et al, 2011). Advisees may initially not see value in advising through social media or online formats and instead prefer face-to-face meetings with advisors. Understandably, what may be useful for advisee/supervisee purposes may differ from advisor/supervisor needs. For instance, faculty may prefer blogs while students use Facebook but ultimately the two could be cross-linked to accommodate everyone (McEachern, 2011).

Social media options offer endless opportunities for faculty, student, and peer collaboration; for enhancement of faculty and student technical abilities; and for increased group cohesion and networking (Melton & Hicks, 2011; Poellhuber et al, 2011). However, these options necessitate the need for faculty, students, and university administration to have the latest updates in order to work simultaneously.

ONLINE ADVISING AND FACULTY WORKLOAD

E-advising, not unlike face-to-face advising, affects faculty workload and subsequent reward structures. Workload needs to be addressed administratively with regard to how much is expected of faculty in their online advising role when social media options are encouraged, supported, and adopted (Luna & Medina, 2007). However, universities while providing ready access cannot drown the students in information overload or overtax faculty. Using various types of media for intended purposes may address this issue so as not to overwhelm advisors/advisees. Smaller advising loads offer a more intimate level of interaction between faculty and advisees and can help situate students more effectively in an advising network (Poellhuber et al, 2011).

Swearingen and Hayes (2009) noted that social media options may facilitate increased contact with advisees in a one-time transmission of information. This may diminish workload issues rather than setting up individual meetings or an on-campus group session to convey information. However, setting up the social media structure may require an infusion of administrative and faculty time.

Tailoring needs to specific populations also requires additional time and effort. Hung and Yuen (2010) encouraged users to adopt a strategic plan and place limits on what and how much social media is used for advising/supervising in order to align with its intended purpose so that it achieves meaningful results. For social media in advising/supervising to be effective, information overload needs to be monitored and time management adjusted accordingly.

Cahn, Benjamin, and Shanahan (2013) suggested tailoring various social media options to be used for faculty development practices. Not only can faculty learn

101

to communicate with graduate advisees, but also graduate schools may provide helpful seminars for faculty advisors on demand, asynchronously through short, streamlined YouTube videos rather than offer them as long face-to-face, all-day seminars. These options can easily fit into tight faculty schedules and be tailored to immediate needs. Professional development offices can also include advisor blogs allowing for ongoing comments and interaction with colleagues.

THE FUTURE OF ONLINE ADVISING

Entre into a new graduate program either traditional or online begins with scanning a graduate program website. Prospective students should be able to view video and audio modules on career planning, interviewing, and applying to that graduate program off the website. For example, Brucato and Neimeyer (2011) found that psychology students who used Virtual Advisor were more actively engaged in their graduate school preparation and increased their self-efficacy compared to non-users. Graduate programs could place some of their basic graduate information and advising resources online for student usage, freeing up valuable advisor time for more individualized professional discussions.

Santilli and Beck (2005) reported that "the majority of faculty time in online courses is spent communicating with students, building and sustaining learning communities" (p. 159). Students are in contact with faculty more in online courses than they are in traditional face-to-face courses. As such, learning communities emerge in online programs to provide students with a "perceived sense of classroom community" (Hung & Yuen, 2010, p. 706) that can extend beyond the classroom. Domizi (2013) found evidence that students appreciated their ability to stay connected and build community. Media usage helped overcome isolation associated with being in graduate school and served to decrease the social and psychological distance traditionally found between advisors, advisees, and peers. Domizi discovered that using social media prompted up-to-the-minute announcements and reminders, added flexibility and continuity to advising, clarified misunderstandings with policy and procedures, and facilitated a community of learners as well as a community of practice.

Social media offers options that combine online formats with social networking options and an opportunity to sustain community. In other words, some online course management systems, while able to facilitate interclass communication, cannot as yet include other students or be available to students when courses end. For instance, NING goes beyond the classroom features of Blackboard (Hung & Yuen, 2010) to sustain community beyond the semester. Until such time as course management systems offer social media options, multiple approaches may be necessary to facilitate greater communication with advisees after classes end.

In conceptualizing the dissertation, electronic publication and access through University Microfilms International (UMI) allow traditional dissertation formats to incorporate hypertext, thus allowing them to move away from the traditional linear print mode. The richness of adding materials to dissertations may be unlimited as technology expands. While electronic means of presentation can enhance old linear dissertation modes, they also suggest opportunities for advisors to encourage students to ask more intriguing questions that advances in technology can help solve as well as illustrate beyond the one-dimensional printed thesis/dissertation (Lang, 2002).

Advisors may feel uncomfortable with these new technological approaches. However, faculty needs to be prepared to develop a greater comfort level with technology in order to advance their field. Furthermore, advisors will need to understand how and when online formats and social media can be used for orientation information, announcing program changes and updates, learning community formation, dissertation formats, and data gathering. To do so means, however, that new skills will need to be added to the advisor's toolkit in order to ensure adequate advising and supervision. Campus administration must be poised to provide these necessary skills.

BEST PRACTICES

- Communication with advisees should be clear, professional, frequent, and tailored to student needs incorporating multiple modes and methods to appropriately match the message.
- Allow students to suggest how social media can be utilized for advising/supervising. Enlisting their expertise to help in that utilization should encourage greater usage.
- Develop advising teams/learning communities through webpages and social media. An online advisor/advisees interaction blog can be augmented with alumni input. Current students can ask alumni questions about the program, thesis/dissertation related issues, and jobs.
- Workshops that promote good faculty advising should include information on the effects of advisor verbal and non-verbal immediacy so that faculty can be cognizant of the implications of immediacy in interaction with all advisees. These workshops might best be delivered electronically and cover a variety of topics in short, easily accessible audio/video modules.
- Create advising plans with department chairs to acknowledge the time and effort devoted to online advising. Faculty and chairs should monitor how the workload differs from traditional advising.
- Social media and online options usage should serve as supplemental to, not a substitute for, traditional faculty advising (Smailes & Gannon-Leary, 2011). Di Pierro (2013) suggested not totally abandoning the traditional "one-on-one consistent engagement with students" in favor or more modern technological methods (p. 32). In online programs face-to-face encounters can always take place virtually.

103

RESOURCES

- Check the course management systems used by your university (Blackboard, eCollege, Moodle, or Sakai) and learn their capabilities regarding social media use. Explore the possibilities associated with using them for advising purposes.
- Blogging and posting of a personal and professional nature includes options such as Bebo, Elgg, Facebook, NING, Orkut, and LinkedIn. Choosing from these options should be based upon advisor/supervisor preferences, advisee/supervisee preferences, and what is supported by your university.
- For microblogging try Flickr, Instagram, or Twitter.
- For web-conferencing try Adobe Connect, E-Luminate, Skype, or WebX. Check on their availability through your IT department.
- The story behind this link www.saem.org/membership/services/e-advising (retrieved April 10, 2014) can be found in Coates et al (2004) and provides an example regarding advisor/advisee online pairings that was used in emergency medicine.

REFERENCES

Bazzoni, J. (2000). The electronic internship advisor: The case for asynchronous communication. *Business Communication Quarterly*, *63*, 101–111.

Beitz, N. (1987). Academic advisement for distance education students. *Journal of Education for Library and Information Science*, *27*, 279–287.

Bocchi, J., Eastman, J., & Swift, K. (2004). Profile of students in an online MBA program and implications for teaching them. *Journal of Education for Business*, *79*, 245–254.

Brucato, B., & Neimeyer, G. (2011). Effectiveness of an online graduate preparation program. *Teaching of Psychology*, *38*, 166–172.

Cahn, P., Benjamin, E., & Shanahan, C. (2013). "Uncrunching time": Medical schools' use of social media for faculty development. *Medical Education Online*, *18*, 20995.

Camacho, M., & Guilana, S. (2011). From personal to social: Learning environments that work. *Digital Education Review*, *20*, 24–36.

Charsky, D., Kish, M., Briskin, J., Hathaway, S., Walsh, K., & Barajas, N. (2009). Millenials need training, too: Using communication technology to facilitate teamwork. *TechTrends: Linking Research and Practice to Improve Learning*, *53*(6), 42–48.

Coates, W., Ankel, F., Birnbaum, A., Kosiak, D., Broderick, K., Thomas, S., Leschke, R., & Collings, J. (2004). The virtual advisor program: Linking students to mentors via the World Wide Web. *Academic Emergency Medicine*, *11*(3), 253–255.

Curry, R., Baldwin, R., & Sharpe, M. (1998). Academic advising in baccalaureate distance education programs. *American Journal of Distance Education*, *12*(3), 42–52.

Di Pierro, M. (2013). Strategies for doctoral student retention: Taking the roads less traveled. *Journal for Quality and Performance*, *35*(3), 29–32.

Domizi, D. (2013). Microblogging to foster connections and community in a weekly graduate seminar course. *TechTrends: Linking Research and Practice to Improve Learning*, *57*(1), 43–51.

Draves, W. (2002). *Teaching online* (2nd ed.). River Falls, WI: LERN Books.

Fornshell, G. (1993). Academic advising for distance learners. *Journal of Instructional Delivery Systems*, *7*(3), 17–19.

Granovetter, M. (1973). The strength of weak ties. *American Journal of Sociology*, *78*, 1360–1380.

Hung, H., & Yuen, S. (2010). Educational use of social networking technology in higher education. *Teaching in Higher Education*, *15*, 703–714.

Jain, S., & Maxson, E. (2011). More about on-line forums for students and faculty. *American Medicine*, *86*, 921.

Janes, D. (2006). Together alone: What students need from an e-moderator. *Canadian Journal of University Continuing Education*, *32*(2), 93–108.

Junco, R., Heibergert, G., & Loken, E. (2011). The effect of Twitter on college student engagement and grades. *Journal of Computer Assisted Learning*, *27*, 119–132.

Kim, K., Liu, S., & Bonk, C. (2005). Online MBA students' perceptions of online learning: Benefits, challenges, and suggestions. *Internet and Higher Education*, *8*, 335–344.

Lang, S. (2002). Electronic dissertations: Preparing students for our past and their futures. *College English*, *64*, 680–695.

Lanier, M. (2006). Academic integrity and distance learning. *Journal of Criminal Justice Education*, *17*, 244–261.

Lave, J., & Wenger, E. (1991). *Situated learning: Legitimate peripheral participation*. Cambridge: Cambridge University Press.

Li, X. (2012). Weaving social media into a business proposal project. *Business Communication Quarterly*, *75*, 68–75.

Lindbeck, R., & Fodrey, B. (2010). Using technology in undergraduate admission: A student perspective. *Journal of College Admission*, *208*, 10–17.

Luke, M., & Gordon, C. (2011). A discourse analysis of school counseling supervisory e-mail. *Counseling Education and Supervision*, *50*, 274–291.

Luna, G., & Medina, C. (2007). Promising practices and challenges: E-advising special education rural graduate students. *Rural Special Education Quarterly*, *26*(4), 21–26.

McEachern, R. (2011). Experiencing a social network in an organizational context: The Facebook internship. *Business Communication Quarterly*, *74*, 486–493.

Mehrabian, A. (1971). *Silent messages*. Belmont, CA: Wadsworth.

Melton, J., & Hicks, N. (2011). Integrating social and traditional media in the client project. *Business Communication Quarterly*, *74*, 494–504.

Metzger, A., Finley, K., Unbrich, T., & McAuley, J. (2010). Pharmacy faculty members' perceptions on the student/faculty relationship in online social networks. *American Journal of Pharmaceutical Education*, 74(10), article 188.

Poellhuber, B., Roy, N., & Anderson, T. (2011). Distance students' readiness for social media and collaboration. *The International Review of Research in Open and Distance Learning*, *12*(6), 102–125.

Richardson, P., MacRae, A., Schwartz, K., Bankston, L., & Kosten, C. (2008). Student outcomes in a post-professional online masters'-degree program. *The American Journal of Occupational Therapy*, *62*, 600–610.

Sacks, M., & Graves, N. (2012). How many "friends" do you need? Teaching students how to network using social media. *Business Communication Quarterly*, *75*, 80–88.

Santilli, S., & Beck, V. (2005). Graduate faculty perceptions of online teaching. *The Quarterly Review of Distance Education*, *6*, 155–160.

Scarcia-King, T. (2011). Effective strategies for virtual supervision. In L. Roper (Ed.), *Supporting and supervising mid-level professionals* (pp. 55–67). New Directions for Student Services no. 136. Hoboken, NJ: Wiley Periodicals.

Smailes, J., & Gannon-Leary, P. (2011). Peer mentoring–Is a virtual form of support a viable alternative? *Research in Learning Technology*, *19*, 129–142.

Swearingen, C., & Hayes, J. (2009). Faculty advising in nursing education: Necessary evil or opportunity for excellence? *International Journal of Nursing Education Scholarship*, 6(1), article 29.

Tay, E., & Allen, M. (2011). Designing social media into university learning: Technology of collaboration or collaboration for technology. *Educational Media International*, *48*, 151–163.

Taylor, M., Jowi, D., Schreier, H., & Bertelsen, D. (2004). Students' perceptions of e-mail interaction during student–professor advising sessions: The pursuit of inter-personal goals. *Journal of Computer-Mediated Communication*, *16*, 307–330.

Wrench, J., & Punyanunt, N. (2004). Advisee–advisor communications: An exploratory study examining interpersonal communication variables in the graduate advisor–advisee relationship. *Communication Quarterly*, *52*, 224–236.

Chapter 8

Chaperoning the Dance

Chairing Thesis and Dissertation Research

Cahn (1994) and Gardner, Hayes, and Neider (2007) regarded the thesis/dissertation chair role as a critical area of responsibility in terms of overseeing the socialization and professionalization processes of advisees. Luebs, Fredrickson, Hyon, and Samraj (1998) delineated three basic duties of the faculty chair: shaping a student's dissertation research, analyzing student work during the dissertation, and preparing the student for academic life or a scholar practitioner role after graduation. Chaperoning the dance describes how faculty guides students from assembling a helpful committee, to stating a good research problem, to formulating research questions, and finally preparing drafts. To develop a good thesis/dissertation hinges on the deepening of the faculty/student relationship and balancing the fiduciary advisor role with the power differential as students move from novice to independent scholar.

REALITIES OF THE CHAIR ROLE

Not every faculty member has the opportunity to chair theses/dissertations because it necessitates research prowess and publication. To be asked to chair, to work with highly competent master's and doctoral students passionate about a cutting-edge topic, however, is worth the time spent with advisees. Even though this working relationship is critical to student success, faculty is seldom trained or receives professional development to perfect it (Smith, Maroney, Nelson, Abel, & Abel, 2006).

Ultimately, chairing becomes a mixed bag of excitement, confusion, gratitude, misunderstanding, satisfaction, ambiguity, clarity, and serendipity. Unfortunately, little normative consensus on how advisees are to be supervised exists (Braxton, Proper, & Bayer, 2011). Various stages in the student's thesis/dissertation mean more or less intensity requiring more or less supervisory oversight, direction, and involvement. Adding to the chaos is the fact that the chairing relationship may be influenced by gender, race, ethnicity, religion, and other factors further complicating and muddying those boundaries (Grant, 2003). And, the process may differ slightly with each new student.

CHAIR/ADVISEE FIDUCIARY RELATIONSHIP

Chair/advisee relationships fluidly move between formal and informal. For formal matters, codes of conduct should exist. As for the informal matters, disciplinary norms and expectations and academic department cultural mores should establish boundaries. However, each chair has a specific set of expectations honed over time.

Because of the special knowledge held by faculty, their tenure, and a demonstrated publication record, faculty is entrusted with certain higher-level academic expectations and earns the distinction of overseeing thesis/dissertation research. While chairs discharge this duty without fear of constant scrutiny, they do so with some measure of normative control or restraint (Parsons & Platt, 1973) as the fate of students lies solely in the hands of the faculty who sits on the dissertation committee.

Therefore, a fiduciary relationship exists. However, the chair/advisee relationship resembles neither a lord/serf association nor a producer/consumer connection. It is rather a status-laden obligation (Parsons & Platt, 1973), so any attempt to create a more democratic relationship between chair and advisee challenges the stratified nature of the role. However, chairs must demonstrate a fiduciary responsibility for the student's welfare. In return, the student accepts a degree of dependence upon the chair (Wolfe & Snock, 1964). Especially at the doctoral level, faculty's fiduciary expectation "carries with it responsibility for integrity, development, and implementation of knowledge . . . [manifest in a] . . . faithful discharge of fiduciary duty" (Parsons & Platt, 1973, p. 130). Furthermore, Parsons and Platt contended that faculty requires autonomy not bureaucratic control in order to function as knowledge creators and advisors of graduate students. Being this is not a "contractual market" type of relationship, the expectation then becomes instead a mutual, committed association of professional chair and novice scholar. Often these budding scholars eventually become valued colleagues with whom faculty participate in future collaborative research projects.

In the fiduciary chair/apprentice model, chairs guide apprentices through the process while the apprentice explores the rigors, parameters, ethics, and joys of developing original research (Reybold, Brazer, Schrum, & Corda, 2012). Students respect faculty expertise which results in mutual trust (Wolfe & Snock, 1964). The relationship will be further characterized by the demands chairs place on their students and the interpretation of those demands by the students as necessary to thesis/dissertation completion. Metaphorically, novice thesis/dissertation students set sail on an intellectual journey (Kottkamp, 2005). The chair navigates with the student until the accomplished student steers his/her own vessel. However, balance must exist between a student's need for independence and his/her tacit reliance on the chair's advice and counsel (Brown & Krager, 1985).

MINIMIZING POWER DIFFERENTIALS IN THE FIDUCIARY RELATIONSHIP

Faculty possesses *personal* power as a result of gaining knowledge of their discipline. Faculty possesses *positional* power by virtue of the graduate faculty status conferred upon them by their institution which is tied to their continued research in their discipline/field. Of these professional powers taken together, the former is used collegially in professional settings while the latter is strictly used over students and related specifically to student theses/dissertation work (Chiang, 2009; Schniederjans, Schniederjans, & Levy, 2012). Chiang found that a positional power stance illuminates a power differential that can stall the student's progress while personal power tends to lean more to collaborative and productive efforts between chair and student. Grant (2003) illustrated that social power differentials seem to be thought of as flowing one way, from chair to advisee, but she wanted students to acknowledge and exercise their own power by treating the document and interaction with the chair seriously, and the chair respecting the student as an emerging independent scholar.

Using French and Raven's (1960) taxonomy of power, Aquinis, Nesler, Quigley, Suk, and Tedeschi (1996) depicted the delicate balance of the ideal chair as possessing high referent, expert, and reward power and low legitimate and coercive power. For instance, when a faculty chair takes weeks to return a draft, it may be rationalized as expert power by the faculty member and legitimate power by the department, but the student may see it as coercive (Abdennur, 2000). Therefore, faculty needs to be more accountable. Turnaround time should be minimal and discussed with the student in advance as to whether the task will be completed in a few days to a week or if it will take much longer. Setting schedules or timetables that faculty advisors and their students agree upon should be set early in the chair/advisee relationship. If the department has guidelines for such matters, it would be easier to establish those expectations but in their absence, chair and advisee should do this together (Bowen & Rudenstine, 1992).

One aspect of the chair role includes pastoral care for which faculty rarely receives training, especially when advising, supervising, chairing the dissertation, and mentoring minority students (Adams, 1986). Some faculty members are reluctant or unable to provide pastoral care because the depth and direction of pastoral care does not fit their experience and/or personality.

However, faculty fears that over involvement might jeopardize the faculty/student relationship (Hockey, 1995) even though giving of one's time

109

proves to be extremely important (Faison, 1996). Instead Shambaugh (2000) advocated that chairs guide students in ways that encompass human sensibility in order to cultivate collaboration and self-reflection. Shambaugh proposed that faculty record their own advising efforts and students assemble a portfolio of their own work. Through these, each party can know the other and what each brings to the relationship academically and personally. Inadvertently, this produces a departmental database over time that can be helpful to chairs and advisors.

CHARACTERIZING THE CHAIR/ADVISOR ROLE

Shopping for the Perfect T-test

Steve knew that he wanted to use only the t-test to analyze his data (irrespective of the research questions) and he made that clear to whomever he spoke. When he pitched his research topic to Professor Kirk, Kirk thought the research problem and question sounded more qualitative in nature. Steve responded that his statistics professor said a t-test was perfectly acceptable. Meeting next with Professor Searle, Steve pitched his topic but Searle wondered how Steve would be able to make group comparisons so t-tests would be inappropriate. Steve reminded Searle that his stats professor told him that he could use a t-test in a dissertation. Professor Lucarelli heard the same pitch and noted that it would be difficult to answer the research question posed no matter what approach was used. Steve returned to stats teacher, Professor Walko to confirm that doing a t-test would suffice to complete the dissertation requirements and Walko said yes. Needless to say it took Kirk, Searle, and Lucarelli a month following a water cooler meeting with Walko to realize that Steve was simply shopping for a chair and his criterion was their acceptance of the t-test.

Beatty (2001) reminded us that students, like Steve, "shop" for the dissertation chair who possesses some knowledge of the student's proposed topic. Not surprising, this is because the thesis/dissertation chair will be paramount in the student's completion of the degree and perhaps instrumental in subsequent job placement (Main, 2014; Spaulding & Rockman-Szapkiew, 2012). Beatty recognized that chair advising style can affect the process and the outcome depending upon whether the advisor is aloof, laissez-faire, hands-on, directive, micromanaging, or simply unavailable.

Lambeth (2008) illustrated seven of eight advising styles that characterize faculty chairs: engaged collaborator, supporter/encourager, technical advisor, popular but overwhelmed favorite, never satisfied, adversarial, and/or absentee chair. Stylizations may overlap or change depending upon the ongoing chair/advisee relationship and the chair's own personal disposition (www.grad.illinois. edu/events/mentoring/2006/advising_styles.htm, retrieved April 16, 2014).

From their study, Knox, Burkhard, Janacek, Pruitt, Fuller, and Hill (2011) characterized chair roles as encompassing cheerleader, counselor, and critic. Faculty shaped student ideas/topics, ensured quality in research and writing, and lent emotional support. Good chair/advisee relationships hinged on a strong professional connection. By contrast, problematic/tense relationships signaled minimal involvement, personality conflicts, frustrations, and eventually changing chairs.

Faculty should determine where students are developmentally. They must assess how much time they have to spend with students and if they possess the level of expertise and interest necessary to chair a particular thesis/dissertation topic (Brown & Krager, 1985). Professors Kirk, Searle, and Lucarelli saw that Steve's grasp of research design and statistics would pose future problems.

CHAIR AS RISK TAKER

The thesis/dissertation advisor is "the single most important micro-environmental factor in [student] success or failure" (Lovitts, 2008, p. 316). Strauss (1964) acknowledged that the faculty member as chair may, on the one hand, grow too close to the student or, on the other hand, remain too far away and fail to advise well. Either chairs possess the willingness to help the student to succeed or maintain a tacit indifference or neglect that eventually portends student failure. Ironically, some faculty nurtures and guides while others dictate and micromanage. Chairs either encourage students to take the lead or cause apprehension. Some students receive little direction from chairs. Some chairs encourage risk taking while offering support, trust, and guidance (Kottkamp, 2005; Ridenour & Twale, 2005). By the same token, some faculty safe in their academic comfort zones (research paradigms, exclusive topics) seldom take risks (alternative theoretical perspectives and research paradigms) or encourage and support their graduate students in risk taking (hot button issues, understudied populations or topics) (Ridenour & Twale, 2005). Some students like Steve fear risk taking and fail to grow, so they select comfortable topics rather than challenge their own boundaries or tackle a new problem of significant concern to the profession.

While students are immersing themselves in the research process, chairs, over the course of their careers, gain other benefits from the experience. Chairing and serving on committees contributes to faculty self-efficacy and professional identity, further socializes them into the faculty role as researcher and advisor, and often exposes them to university politics through which they must maneuver on behalf of their students (Reybold et al, 2012). Chairing theses/dissertation places chairs in new roles. It expands their capabilities with each student whose unique research they guide, assuming they are willing to take risks and move beyond their own boundaries.

ON BECOMING A THESIS/DISSERTATION CHAIR

Main (2014) used the term *homophily* to illustrate that persons prefer to group together in similar social networks. As such, female doctoral students paired with female faculty chairs/advisors more often than they did with male advisors and, conversely, male students paired more often with male chairs/advisors. As a result of greater communication and regular meetings with their female chairs/advisors, these women increased their chances of being supported psychologically, internalizing the norms of their profession, and graduating. Chair/advisee pairings are critical.

In addition, greater responsibilities above and beyond what the basic advising role entails come with each semester that the advisee progresses to the thesis/dissertation defense. It requires the chair to employ a new or modified skill set commensurate with student needs for completion of that stage (Schniederjans et al, 2012). This becomes especially critical when chairing theses/dissertations of underrepresented student groups and international students (Liechty, Schull, & Liao, 2009).

Knox et al (2011) suggested that chairs and advisees discuss expectations with each other including "advising work style, interpersonal patterns, research competencies and motivation, perceptions of each other's roles, level of monitoring sought or needed, and preferred mode of communication" (p. 67). Knowing turnaround time on drafts and subsequent revisions should also be included (Schniederjans et al, 2012). Because faculty new to chairing may not know how best to proceed, effective advising may be one thing to discuss with one's department chair and one's own career mentor.

FORMULATING THE PLAN OF STUDY

Who Needs an Advisor?

Professor Dietrich sat down with Karen to help her complete her doctoral plan of study. She needed to take several required courses but she informed Dietrich that she did not want to take them from two of the professors teaching them. With both professors well respected in their field and highly published, Dietrich sat perplexed at her request. Karen suggested instead that Dietrich offer those courses to her as independent studies under his guidance. Karen lived at a distance from the university and held a full-time job so this alternative would work better for her. She agreed to take other required classes on campus just not the required ones offered by those two professors. Dietrich agreed reluctantly to sign the plan of study form and offer to her those four courses as independent studies.

Serving as a contract for the university and a guide for students, plans of study should be done as soon after orientation as feasible. Plans of study can list more than just a course sequence, chair, and committee members. Space should also be allotted for student research opportunities, attending conferences, and completing internships, practicums, clinicals, residencies, assistantships, and/or fellowships. Faculty needs to convey to students that receiving the degree entails more than just taking classes and writing a thesis/dissertation (Shambaugh, 2000). The plan of study should depict all the elements of their multidimensional socialization process (Weidman, Twale, & Stein, 2001). Life can change between matriculation and defense, so changes in plans of study are to be expected. However, circumventing the system to accommodate a student's schedule, idiosyncrasies, or preferences may do students like Karen a grave injustice in the long run.

FORMING THE COMMITTEE

Ideally, thesis/dissertation committees spark ideas and clarify them through convergence and collaboration as well as serve to refine the research process (Buraway, 2005). Selecting committee members, however, can have academic, social, and political implications. Crum and Franklin (2002) learned that females assigned to chairs and committees expressed dismay compared to those permitted to form their own committees. Consequently, chairs should offer students suggestions for inside and outside members but the final selection should be the student's. This principle holds also for changes along the journey to the degree (Schniederjans et al, 2012). Freeman and Loadman (1985) found that those who included a faculty member well versed in research methods and/or statistics offered a more positive rating of their doctoral experience than those students who did not.

BECOMING A COMMITTEE MEMBER

Faculty tends to learn thesis/dissertation advising over time and on the job rather than from receiving formal training. Reybold et al (2012) learned that faculty serving on committees had little knowledge of procedure, commitment, or participation expectations beyond what they experienced in their own dissertation defense. This may be compounded by the presence of outside members on the committee whose departments view thesis/dissertation research differently or who adopt different procedures for defense protocol.

Furthermore, it would be considered unprofessional for faculty to criticize colleagues' judgment regarding the oversight of graduate student research. Faculty respects colleagues' work and hesitates to challenge peers even when it might be in the best interest of the student and the chair (Campbell, 2000; Mieczkowski,

1995). Committee membership should be a stimulating and provocative learning experience not a chore.

Damrosch (1995) questioned if faculty *can* work together in student-assembled committees of faculty, especially if members view the student's topic from different subspecialties and perspectives. Oftentimes, faculty in the same discipline, field, or program disagrees on what constitutes good research or a good dissertation (Latterell, 2002). Some practitioner fields and degrees conferred will suggest more applied research designs and/or value a professional team approach. Ultimately, this will require significant adjustments in collaboration with practicing professionals from the field either working in person or in online formats (Fink, 2006). Faculty new to professional team approaches should serve on a committee before attempting to chair one.

Junior faculty members may also be guarded in their committee participation especially if they are inside committee members. These members learn from other colleagues on the committee and even co-chair a few as they gain savvy in preparation for eventually chairing alone (Bowen & Rudenstine, 1992). In fact, Reybold et al (2012) described committee participation as "a display of professional expertise" and for junior faculty a facet of the developmental academic culture (p. 239). Junior faculty of color may find they must show deeper investment in the committee process to ensure their input is valued. When unsure about something, junior faculty should solicit the input of another valued committee member (Beatty, 2001).

ADVICE ON TOPIC SELECTION, RESEARCH PROBLEM, RESEARCH QUESTIONS, AND METHOD

Isaac, Quinlan, and Walker (1992) reported that students often experience difficulty selecting and conceptualizing a thesis/dissertation topic. As students contemplate their topic and research problem and propose it to their chair, Beatty (2001) suggested that the chair's response should be, "who cares" or "so what." Not to be flippant or disrespectful, but the point is to bring the student to the realization that the thesis/dissertation should be unique and original. Students should explore a problem whose answers make a contribution to the literature in the field/discipline as well as to the group under study. These probing questions represent a means to broaden a narrow topic or make a narrow one into a manageable size. Lastly, the chair needs to assess if the research is actually achievable given time, student budget constraints, and the methodology(s) chosen.

Mendenhall (1983) contended that advisors should have interest in the student's topic, be accessible and available, guide the student in topic selection and refinement, and assess student research skill level. He suggested matching students' research designs to their level of expertise as a way to help students gain confidence as independent scholars, minimize frustration, and promote their intellectual development. This may explain why some students like Steve gravitate to advisors who seemingly do not challenge their limitations but instead convey that scholarly research is easy and simplistic. Some, though not all faculty, would agree that we do students and the discipline a disservice by allowing them to hover in the comfort/no-risk zone by not challenging students (and the chair) to reach higher aspirations with their scholarship.

ADVICE ON COMPILING THE PROPOSAL/PROSPECTUS

The *prospectus* is a guide to dissertation research, that is, a malleable, expandable beginning (Benesh, 2001; Buraway, 2005). However, a *proposal* can be as extensive as the first three chapters of the thesis/dissertation. The format tends to vary by department, school, university, field/discipline, and/or chair. The advisor decides how lengthy the proposal should be and when the document is ready to be informally viewed by or formally presented to the whole committee (Beatty, 2001).

The prospectus/proposal overview meeting of all parties should be a scheduled formality but conducted informally and collegially to allow for collaborative synthesis. Committee comments must be helpful and encouraging not paralyzing and confusing (Beatty, 2001; Benesh, 2001; Buraway, 2005). Commentary should include recommendations and suggested changes (additions, deletions, clarifications) regarding methodology, research questions, instrumentation, design, data collection, and statistical procedures in order to refine the document before the student proceeds any further. However, the benefits to having the first three chapters approved by the committee takes away a tremendous burden from the student as well as the chair before the final defense. Candidates need to focus on completing the data gathering and the content of the last two chapters rather than also wondering about the approval of the first three during the defense.

Over a chair's career, various topics and methodologies have been supervised. These defended dissertations serve as resources and guides for current students (Knox et al, 2011). Proposal writing workshops and mini-symposiums by faculty and doctoral candidates may be helpful to students and faculty advisors as attendees share advice and offer critique and suggestions for improvement (Wasby, 2001). These may be critical retention considerations for administrators as the proposal is a major hurdle for the student and one that stymies forward progress to the degree.

PROVIDING FEEDBACK ON THESIS/DISSERTATION DRAFTS

Ahmad (2007) described the dissertation advisor's duty as offering support and suggestions, helping the student set boundaries, but then allowing the student to conduct his or her research. He characterized the dissertation research process as allowing the student to be lost in the data so that the student can demonstrate competence to explore and discover which way to best present and interpret it rather than for the advisor to just complete the process for the struggling advisee.

Therefore, a chair's written feedback on drafts goes beyond grammar and punctuation to encompass helping the student reach the goal of being an independent scholar and fulfilling the expectations of the academic community (Bitchener, Basturkmen, & East, 2010). Supportive verbal feedback should also increase the student's motivation to continue, especially when it is communicated frequently, in a timely fashion, and is helpful to learning (Jaama & Koper, 1998).

Chair feedback differs based on content, discipline/field, and student ability but includes five basic areas: (1) *content*—presence/absence of relevant/irrelevant theory and research studies, gaps in the literature review, clear understanding of major concepts and constructs, inappropriate inclusion of personal opinion; (2) *organization*—appropriate placement of specific material in specific chapters and in rational order; (3) *structure*—grammar, sentence structure, idea development in paragraphs, transitions, flow, confusing passages; (4) *cohesion*—writing quality, subheadings, easy-to-follow charts, graphs, conceptual models, and illustrations, easy-to-follow technical writing style; and (5) *accuracy*—technical vocabulary choices, inclusion of studies and their proper interpretation, and simplistic, technical language to convey the correct meaning (Bitchener et al, 2010).

Draft feedback should be clear and focus on how the student can correct the document (Schniederjans et al, 2012). Track changes online versus cursive writing on a hard copy can speed up the process. This method makes it easier to tell *how and where* students addressed chair or committee inquiry without having to remember, cross-check, or reread everything again. Also ESL students can easily translate wordprocessed chair comments into their native language for easier, more efficient communication. It allows for follow-up of non-responsiveness to or misinterpretations of comments by either party. Asking students to highlight changes in the document helps chairs/committee members locate them more easily in subsequent drafts.

Seasoned faculty chairs realize that some students tend to be more mature than others and thus capable of greater independence and less direction. Because each chair/advisee relationship is different, chairing a committee varies by case, therefore it becomes difficult for faculty to be prepared for each new challenge (Compton-Hall, 2002). The goal of the faculty chair is to work with each type of student to produce an independent scholar with a defensible document.

Thesis/dissertation writing confounds many students as it appears much less clear than did explicit coursework assignments and comprehensive examination questions. Because the nature of dissertation writing is unique and different for the student, chairs calling for additions and revisions probably appear to the student as overwhelming, impossible, demanding ogres. Compton-Hall (2002) noted

116

that, as a result, students do not often follow the directives given by the thesis/dissertation chair. Therefore, when chairs offer suggestions and guidance to students who fail to accept them, chairs may shy from offering further assistance to those students (Krueger & Peek, 2006). In any event, chairs must understand and persevere.

ADMINISTRATIVE ADVICE TO PROGRAM COORDINATORS/DIRECTORS AND GRADUATE DEANS

Graduate schools should consider drafting general guidelines for chairs and dissertation committee members that aim to create and sustain effective relationships. These allow faculty to take the chair role more seriously (Austin & McDaniels, 2006; Cahn, 1994).

Valid and reliable instruments that measure advising/chairing outcomes are needed to formulate better guidelines for assisting chairs, committees, and students (Barnes, Chard, Wolfe, Stassen, & Williams, 2011). These instruments should also include ways to measure perceptions of the departmental climate in terms of how chairing relates to student success.

Departments would be prudent to keep more extensive records on their thesis/dissertation students. Administratively, chairs need to apprise the registrar and/or program director when the "all but dissertation or thesis" student is not making satisfactory progress to the degree and why. Periodically, graduate school administrators should be encouraged to examine time to degree statistics for doctoral students. If the time is longer than what would be considered normal, which varies with each program, or if some programs incur greater numbers of stop outs, monitoring this could provide some answers to attrition. Answers may be obtained during exit interviews or periodic checking on students who have stopped out in order to ascertain their reasons for leaving and not returning. Gathering this information would best be done by a neutral graduate school administrator rather than the department to increase the likelihood that students would be forthcoming with their experiences and reasons for dropping or stopping out of their program following candidacy.

Chairs need to be apprised by administration of available campus resources located in the graduate school, one's own college, and domestic and international student services that benefit all graduate students, particularly underrepresented, at-risk, and non-native populations (Knox et al, 2011).

Faculty rewards approximate organizational values. When organizational values favor research over teaching and service, chairing tends to hold a lesser value even though it may be professionally significant albeit time consuming (Diamond, 1993). Without incentives and rewards, many faculty offer to do minimal thesis/dissertation chairing even though chairing factors into their workload, not to mention providing intrinsic professional benefits. In many departments, the

117

extrinsic rewards remain elusive but intrinsic satisfaction is considered priceless by the administration and rewarded comparably. Unfortunately reward systems often do not recognize mid- and late-career faculty who are ideally suited to direct graduate student research.

Among those departments that do acknowledge thesis/dissertation chairing duties as significant, reward systems still vary by department and school. Chairs may receive a stipend for each successful defense. In other departments, a specific number of dissertations to be defended in a specific term or semester may qualify the chair for a course release.

BEST PRACTICES

Faculty Purview

- Program faculty should meet regularly to discuss student progress and problems with student thesis/dissertation research to prevent student departure as well as increase faculty collegiality.
- Thesis/dissertation chairs in conjunction with program directors should hold in-person, online or hybrid orientations as candidates enter the dissertation research phase (Crum & Franklin, 2002) so students can reconnect with peers. They can provide candidates with fruitful sessions on expectations, critiquing others' work, offering suggestions and support, and practicing writing the thesis/dissertation discussion section (Bowen & Rudenstine, 1992).
- Encourage social and virtual gatherings and online chat to further maintain collaborative peer networks (Shambaugh, 2000).
- Davidson and Foster-Johnson (2001), Beatty (2001) and Casto, Caldwell, and Salazar (2005) recommended that chairs and advisees document the time they spend together. During the first advising session, chairs should keep a log and encourage advisees to maintain a journal to keep track of time lapses by each party, to note information and suggestions discussed in meetings, and to establish goals that need to be accomplished before the next meeting.
- Chairs could suggest students attend counseling workshops to discuss common issues students have about the dissertation phase. Counseling departments could offer seminars on stress management and coping strategies to assist students with social, physical, personal, peer, and academic matters (Smith et al, 2006; Davis, Eshelman, & McKay, 2000).

Administrative Purview

- University-wide training workshops for faculty chairs on dissertation policies and procedures and advising strategies and role responsibilities should be offered each year (Liechty et al, 2009). Universities might consider offering workshops on chairing different empirical research styles, taking risks, and working with diverse student populations (Di Pierro, 2007; Ridenour & Twale, 2005).

■ Departments need to conduct performance evaluations of chairs to monitor how many advisees faculty can chair at any one time and also how long chair and student(s) take to complete the thesis/dissertation (Bowen & Rudenstine, 1992).

■ Chairing should be addressed in the faculty workload, valued, and comparably rewarded. Faculty awards, rewards, and incentives strengthen the chair role and acknowledge its significance to student progress as well as its contribution to the scholarship of the discipline/field (Diamond, 1993; Liechty et al, 2009).

■ Because doctoral committees influence student retention, assessing thesis/ dissertation committee effectiveness and overall performance can be revealing. Departing students could be asked to compare what they expected against what they received during the completion of their thesis/dissertation (Freeman & Loadman, 1985). Focus groups and exit interviews of underrepresented groups are recommended to help administrations gain more information on how better to chair/advise these student groups.

RESOURCES

■ Green and Kluever's (1997) *Dissertation Barriers Scale,* Kluever and Green's (1998) *The Responsibility Scale* and Winston and Sandor's (1984) *The Academic Advising Inventory* can serve as tools to help faculty and administration target advisor strengths and potential difficulties (www.nacada.ksu.edu/Resources/ Clearinghouse/View-Articles/Academic-Advising-Inventory-.aspx, retrieved April 7, 2014).

■ For information on Duke University's Advisor's Toolkit see Woods, Burgess, Kaminetzky, McNeill, Pinheiro, and Heflin (2010).

■ Luse, Mennecke, and Townsend (2012) provide a useful framework to aid chairs and students with topic section.

REFERENCES

Abdennur, A. (2000). *Camouflaged aggression: The hidden threat to individuals and organizations.* Calgary, Alberta: Detselig Enterprises.

Adams, H. (1986). *Minority participation in graduate education: An action plan.* Report of the National Invitational Forum on the Status of Minority Participation in Graduate Education. Washington, DC. (ERIC Document Reproduction Service No. ED291 272)

Ahmad, K. (2007). *PhD: The pursuit of excellence.* Singapore: Thompson Learning Asia.

Aquinis, H., Nesler, M., Quigley, B., Suk, J., & Tedeschi, J. (1996). Powerbase of faculty supervisors and educational outcomes for graduate students. *Journal of Higher Education, 67,* 267–297.

Austin, A., & McDaniels, M. (2006). Preparing the professoriat of the future: Graduate student socialization for faculty roles. In J. Smart (Ed.), *Higher education handbook of theory and research*, Volume 21 (pp. 397–456). Dordrecht, Netherlands: Springer.

Barnes, B., Chard, L., Wolfe, E., Stassen, M., & Williams, E. (2011). An evaluation of the psychometric properties of the *Graduate Advisory Survey* for doctoral students. *International Journal of Doctoral Studies*, *6*, 1–17.

Beatty, S. (2001). The doctoral supervisor–student relationship: Some American advice for success. *The Marketing Review*, *2*, 205–217.

Benesh, S. (2001). The key to a successful prospectus: Consult an advisor early and often. *PS: Political Science and Politics*, *34*, 853–854.

Bitchener, J., Basturkmen, H., & East, M. (2010). The focus of supervisor written feedback to thesis/dissertation students. *International Journal of English Studies*, *10*(2), 79–98.

Bowen, H., & Rudenstine, N. (1992). *In pursuit of the PhD*. Princeton, NJ: Princeton University Press.

Braxton, J., Proper, E., & Bayer, A. (2011). *Professors behaving badly*. Baltimore: Johns Hopkins University Press.

Brown, R., & Krager, L. (1985). Ethical issues in graduate education: Faculty and student responsibilities. *Journal of Higher Education*, *56*, 403–418.

Buraway, M. (2005). Combat in the dissertation zone. *American Sociologist*, *36*(2), 42–56.

Cahn, S. (1994). *Saints and scamps*. Lanham, MD: Rowman & Littlefield.

Campbell, J. (2000). *Dry rot in the ivory tower*. Lanham, MD: University Press of America.

Casto, C., Caldwell, C., & Salazar, C. (2005). Creating mentoring relationships between female faculty and students in counselor education: Guidelines for potential mentees and mentors. *Journal of Counseling & Development*, *83*, 331–336.

Chiang, S. (2009). Personal power and positional power in a power-full "I": A discourse analysis of doctoral dissertation supervision. *Discourse and Communication*, *3*, 255–272.

Compton-Hall, M. (2002). Mentoring in parallel universes. *Reading Psychology*, *23*, 145–158.

Crum, C., & Franklin, K. (2002, November). *An exploration of mentoring female graduate students in southern metropolitan universities*. Paper presented at the annual meeting of the Mid-South Educational Research Association, Chattanooga, TN. (ERIC Document Reproduction Service No. ED474 592)

Damrosch, D. (1995). *We scholars: Changing the culture of the university*. Cambridge, MA: Harvard University Press.

Davidson, M., & Foster-Johnson, L. (2001). Mentoring in the preparation of graduate researchers of color. *Review of Educational Research*, *71*, 549–574.

Davis, M., Eshelman, E., & McKay, M. (2000). *The relaxation and stress reduction workbook* (5th ed). Oakland, CA: New Harbinger.

Diamond, R. (1993). Changing priorities and the faculty reward system. In R. Diamond & B. Adam (Eds.), *Recognizing faculty work: Reward systems for the year 2000* (pp. 5–22). New Directions for Higher Education, no. 81. San Francisco: Jossey-Bass.

Di Pierro, M. (2007). Excellence in doctoral education: Defining best practices. *College Student Journal, 41*, 368–375.

Faison, J. (1996, April). *The next generation: The mentoring of African American graduate students on predominantly white campuses.* Paper presented at the annual meeting of the American Educational Research Association, New York. (ERIC Document Reproduction Service No. ED401 344)

Fink, D. (2006). The professional doctorate: Its relativity to the PhD and relevance for the knowledge economy. *International Journal of Doctoral Studies, 1*, 35–43.

Freeman, D., & Loadman, W. (1985). Advice to doctoral guidance committees from alumni from two universities. *Research in Higher Education, 22*, 335–346.

French, J., & Raven, R. (1960). The bases of social power. In D. Cartwright & A. Zander (Eds.), *Group dynamics* (pp. 607–623). New York: HarperCollins.

Gardner, S., Hayes, M., & Neider, X. (2007). The dispositions and skills of a PhD, in education: Perspectives of faculty and graduate students in one College of Education. *Innovative Higher Education, 31*, 287–299.

Grant, B. (2003). Mapping the pleasures and risks of supervision. *Discourse: Studies in the Cultural Politics of Education, 24*, 175–190.

Green, K., & Kluever, R. (1997, March). *The Dissertation Barriers Scale.* Paper presented at the annual meeting of the American Educational Research Association, Chicago. (ERIC Document Reproduction Service No. ED410 253)

Hockey, J. (1995). Getting too close: A problem and possible solutions in social science PhD supervision. *British Journal of Guidance and Counseling, 23*, 199–210.

Isaac, P., Quinlan, S., & Walker, W. (1992). Faculty perspectives of the doctoral dissertation. *Journal of Higher Education, 63*, 241–268.

Jaama, M., & Koper, R. (1998). The relationship of student–faculty out-of-class communication to instructional immediacy and trust to student motivation. *Communication Educator, 48*, 41–47.

Kluever, R., & Green, K. (1998). The Responsibility Scale: A research note on dissertation completion. *Educational and Psychological Measurement, 58*, 520–531.

Knox, S., Burkhard, A., Janacek, J., Pruitt, N., Fuller, S., & Hill, C. (2011). Positive and problematic dissertation experiences: The faculty perspective. *Counseling Psychology Quarterly, 24*, 55–69.

Kottkamp, R. (2005, October). *Doctoral study in educational leadership: Arthur Levine's prescription and reflective questions with democratic implications.* Conversation presented at the annual meeting of the University Council for Educational Administration, Nashville.

Krueger, P., & Peek, L. (2006). Figuring it out: A conversation about how to complete your PhD. *College Student Journal, 40*, 149–157.

121

Lambeth, G. (2008). *Advising styles*. www.grad.illinois.edu/events/mentoring/2006/advising_styles.htm (retrieved April 5, 2014).

Latterell, C. (2002). Dissertation writing and advising in a post-modern age. In N. Welch, C. Latterell, C. Moore, & S. Carter-Todd, *The dissertation and the discipline* (pp. 45–54). Cross Currents: New Perspectives in Rhetoric and Composition. Portsmouth, NH: Boynton/Cook.

Liechty, J., Schull, C., & Liao, M. (2009). Facilitating dissertation completion and success among doctoral students in social work. *Journal of Social Work Education, 45,* 481–498.

Lovitts, B. (2008). The transition to independent research: Who makes it, who doesn't, and why. *Journal of Higher Education, 79,* 295–325.

Luebs, M., Fredrickson, K., Hyon, S., & Samraj, B. (1998). John Swales as mentor: The view from the doctoral group. *English for Specific Purposes, 17,* 67–85.

Luse, A., Mennecke, B., & Townsend, A. (2012). Selecting a research topic: A framework for doctoral students. *International Journal of Doctoral Studies, 7,* 143–152.

Main, J. (2014). Gender homophily, PhD completion, and time to degree in the humanities and humanistic social sciences. *Review of Higher Education, 37,* 349–375.

Mendenhall, M. (1983). Overcoming obstacles in a dissertation requirement: Advice to a doctoral candidate. *Teaching of Psychology, 10,* 210–212.

Mieczkowski, B. (1995). *The rot at the top: Dysfunctional bureaucracy in academe.* Lanham, MD: University Press of America.

Parsons, T., & Platt, G. (1973). *The American university.* Cambridge, MA: Harvard University Press.

Reybold, L.E., Brazer, S.D., Schrum, L., & Corda, K. (2012). The politics of dissertation advising: How early career women faculty negotiate access and participation. *Innovative Higher Education, 37,* 227–242.

Ridenour, C.S., & Twale, D.J. (2005). Academic generations exploring intellectual risk taking in an educational leadership program. *Education, 126,* 158–165.

Schniederjans, D., Schniederjans, M., & Levy, Y. (2012). Equity theory based strategies for students on overcoming problems in the PhD dissertation committee. *International Journal of Doctoral Studies, 7,* 221–233.

Shambaugh, R.N. (2000). Reframing doctoral programs: A program of human inquiry for doctoral students and faculty advisors. *Innovative Higher Education, 24,* 295–308.

Smith, R., Maroney, K., Nelson, K., Abel, A., & Abel, H. (2006). Doctoral programs: Changing high rates of attrition. *Journal of Humanistic Counseling, Education, and Development, 45,* 17–32.

Spaulding, L., & Rockman-Szapkiew, A. (2012). Hearing their voices: Factors doctoral candidates attribute to their persistence. *International Journal of Doctoral Studies, 7,* 199–220.

Strauss, A. (1964). Regularized status-passage. In W. Bennis, E. Schein, D. Berlow, & F. Steele (Eds.), *Interpersonal dynamics* (pp. 409–416). Homewood, IL: Dorsey Press.

Wasby, S. (2001). Introduction: Advising and the dissertation proposal. *PS: Political Science and Politics*, *34*, 841–842.

Weidman, J., Twale, D., & Stein, E. (2001). *Socialization of graduate and professional students in higher education: A perilous passage?* San Francisco: Jossey-Bass.

Winston, R., & Sandor, J. (1984). *The Academic Advising Inventory*. Athens, GA: NACADA.

Wolfe, D., & Snock, J.D. (1964). A study of tensions and adjustment under role conflict. In W. Bennis, E. Schein, D. Berlow, & F. Steele (Eds.), *Interpersonal dynamics* (pp. 431–439). Homewood, IL: Dorsey Press.

Woods, S., Burgess, L., Kaminetzky, C., McNeill, D., Pinheiro, S., & Heflin, M. (2010). Defining the role of advisors and mentors in post graduate medical education: Faculty perceptions, roles, responsibilities, and resource needs. *Journal of Graduate Medical Education*, *2*, 195–200.

Chapter 9

Preparing to Launch

Advising the Professional Rites of Passage

There is nothing more exciting than to watch graduate students give birth to their research ideas. Chairs hold a tacit obligation to shepherd/coach students through the final stages of the program and, like a midwife, provide support, affirmation, and endorsement. Ironically, the fate of graduate students rests solely in the hands of the faculty (Damrosch, 1995; Parsons & Platt, 1973). Madsen (2003) described the irony in these graduate school "rites of passage" this way: "It is a curious club that psychologically bludgeons its prospective members over a long period then smilingly welcomes them into the academic fraternity" (p. 77). As evaluators, chairs must determine when students are ready to launch into each successive stage of their program and into academic or professional practice.

PREPARING STUDENTS FOR ORAL AND WRITTEN COMPS

Oral exams date back to the early colonial college days while written exams emerged in the mid-1800s. Exams external to the university, regulated by professional organizations and government bodies which award certification and licensure through written tests, surfaced in the early 1900s (Brubaker & Rudy, 1997). These testing options measured knowledge comprehension, mastery of disciplinary/field literature, oral and written skills, organization, and the critical thinking skills of analysis, evaluation, and synthesis (Pelfrey & Hague, 2000). Professional area exams assessed additional skill comprehension, procedural assessments, application of theory, and may be administered by multiple examiners (Morris, Gallagher, & Ridgway, 2012).

Comprehensive examination procedures differ across disciplines. They may also be individually specified by faculty committees within a department and change over time (Freeman & Loadman, 1985). Mawn and Goldberg (2012) showed differences between the methods used to evaluate students and the goals and objectives for testing them. Because no one method of evaluation of student mastery of knowledge fits the needs of all programs, "programs adopt multiple approaches to show students' progress, knowledge, and capabilities" (p. 161).

Examination options that move a student to candidacy may include a timed one-, two-, or three-day written examination, take home exam, portfolio, and/or an oral exam. Comprehensives could also be fulfilled with a publishable quality paper or action research project. Subsequently a poster session or conference presentation could be organized when multiple students complete this phase of their program each semester/year (Mawn & Goldberg, 2012; Pelfrey & Hague, 2000). Regardless of the option(s) selected, faculty should look for the degree to which the students answered the questions posed, followed guidelines, and satisfied the upper cognitive and affective levels of Bloom's Taxomony (Bloom, Engehart, Furst, Hill, & Krathwohl, 1984; Krathwohl, Bloom, & Masia, 1964).

Viewing comprehensives as merely a gatekeeping function conflicts with Shambaugh's (2000) concept of enhancing students' "ways of being." He suggests another comprehensive option: Ask students to relate their coursework, program activities, and professional experiences to the research focus of their dissertation and also to professional practice. Cognitive maps constructed and discussed by the student through written or oral narrative help capture their journey through self-reflection. Faculty needs to know to what extent students have internalized and applied aspects of their graduate program so they can know if the students have aligned their values with those of the profession and how they demonstrate this professionally. While this benefits the student, advisors can also use this approach to remedy deficiencies in the graduate program or their own advising style (Shambaugh, 2000).

Building Cohort Relationships

When it came time for a cohort of doctoral students to prepare for their comprehensive examinations, Bev, Judy, Rod, and Terry asked Professor Sekula if he would meet with them at a convenient location off campus on several consecutive weekends prior to the event. They wanted to make sure they synthesized the information expected on the exam and Sekula would be the best person to aid them. He agreed because this group had been wonderful throughout their coursework phase and three of them asked him to chair their dissertations. He viewed this opportunity as a way to create an even stronger bond and ensure that with the extra attention they received, each student would be more likely to be admitted to candidacy and complete their degree on time. These students asked other faculty with whom they worked to attend these meetings as well but the others declined.

Students should not go blindly into their comprehensive examinations without careful faculty scrutiny and guidance. Faculty obligation to their advisees at this critical point in their program tends to distinguish the involved advisors from the less involved advisors. While it may not *always* be possible to shepherd *all* students through their comps given time constraints, advisors/chairs must take interest in students securing candidacy, strengthening their faculty/student relationship, and setting the stage for the commitment of both parties to thesis/dissertation proposal development.

PREPARING STUDENTS FOR THESIS/DISSERTATION DEFENSES

At the conclusion of a graduate program, the defense signifies a culminating activity that certifies "that the recipient had capabilities and training for independent scholarly work" by completing an original project that contributes to the knowledge base in a particular field/discipline (Isaac, Quinlan, & Walker, 1992, p. 241). Although this independently conducted original work reflects good writing skills and research prowess on the part of the candidate, it also reflects heavily on the skills and abilities of the chair and the committee.

Purposes for the oral defense, beyond a significant rite of passage or a quality control mechanism, include mastery of candidate oral presentation skills, subject and research area immediacy (thinking on one's feet), and fielding questions successfully and calmly as practice for conference presentations (Isaac et al, 1992). Triggering student stress and tension, the defense could be the student's first real professional effort. Furthermore, working with seasoned academics could be extremely intimidating (Diamond, 1993; Goodchild & Miller, 1997).

This Rarely Happens

A senior administrator, Dean Rios-Conde, frequently served as an adjunct in the organizational psychology department and agreed to chair Susanne's dissertation. The other committee members were experienced tenured professors in the department. One of those department professors had been Susanne's advisor during her program and they developed a good relationship. On the eve of her defense, Susanne called Professor Ramsey to say she was nervous and needed some encouragement. Having finished reading the document earlier that day, Ramsey kindly but sincerely suggested that from her perspective, the research could not be defended and that it would be in Susanne's best interest to talk to Rios-Conde and postpone the defense. Susanne laughed and said she had already bought plane tickets for her parents to see her walk at fall graduation, so postponement was not an option. During the meeting the next day before the defense officially began, other committee members expressed their concerns about how the research had been inappropriately conducted and reported. Diplomatically and collegially, Rios-Conde broke the news to Susanne before the committee and they proceeded to offer her suggestions to help her strengthen the document so the defense could be rescheduled for the spring semester.

Chairs hope students spend time preparing for their oral defenses. Because oral defenses (vivas) represent a significant aspect of the graduate program and a valid rite of passage, faculty needs to take the obligation more seriously and allot time for their own preparation as well. It remains the chair's responsibility to sort out what may be confusing to the student about the presentation (Grabbe, 2003). Sadly, Dean Rios-Conde allowed the defense to be scheduled without due diligence to carefully scrutinizing the document. Susanne presumed that allowing the defense to be scheduled meant the dissertation *was* defensible. The committee members did their job at the defense, *but* had they been brought into the process sooner, perhaps this unfortunate outcome would never have happened.

Customarily, students are excused from a defense prior to and following it in order for committee members to confer, as in Susanne's case. Initially, faculty exclude the student to make sure the document is defensible and then, later, to determine if the student passed the defense. TWIG (1996) believed this sends a clear message regarding the chair/advisee power differential. According to Isaac et al (1992), faculty sees "no viable alternative to the doctoral dissertation" (p. 249) because change would require different skill sets for the chair and committee. However, ensuring more successful defenses and less power differential is within faculty purview.

In order to avoid what happened to Susanne, Hartley and Fox (2004) recommended faculty coordinate and encourage student participation in a mock oral. They suggested students view a real or staged video of a defense, attend a live defense, or participate in a live practice run of a defense. Faculty needs to prepare students to realize that each defense will vary in length and take on a unique flavor due to committee composition, research topic, and questions posed in the defense. Designed to provide students with anticipatory knowledge of the process, mock or live oral exams should prepare pre-defense students procedurally and emotionally for their own upcoming defense so as to avoid a negative or stressful experience.

Mock defenses can also promote a community of scholars (Church, 2009). Faculty, pre-candidacy students, doctoral candidates, co-workers, alumni, and/or invited guests pose questions to the mock candidate to help them synthesize material and coherently respond to questions. Mock defenses offer participants an opportunity to "publically prepare their research; cope with and responsibly address challenging questions concerning their procedures and findings with confidence and eloquence; anticipate statistical queries and develop plausible alternative responses; and demonstrate a knowledge of appropriate behavior and professional demeanor during the final oral defense" (Church, 2009, p. 314).

In addition to the mock defense option, Arnkoff, Glass, and Robinson (1992) explored student anxiety and performance outcomes in dissertation defenses. They recommended university counseling centers offer a twice yearly workshop for students preparing for defenses. While anxiety did not predict cognitive student performance, Arnkoff et al. believed less anxious defenders would value the defense as a professional educational experience rather than a harrowing ordeal or a hoop through which to jump.

INTRODUCING STUDENTS TO THE ACADEMIC COMMUNITY, CONFERENCE ATTENDANCE, AND PRESENTATIONS

Through socialization processes and observing mentors, master's and doctoral students can acknowledge the "pecking order" common to their field (Nettles & Millett, 2006). Professional capital can be stored through conference presentations, published articles in refereed, non-refereed, or practitioner publications; book chapters; and scholarly books. Increasing student capital while in the graduate program does not go unnoticed by the faculty or prospective employers.

In order to introduce students to the academic community, advisors/supervisors should accompany their graduate advisees/supervisees to local, regional, national, and/or international conferences in order for students to see how the profession functions, how new research is introduced, how proposals are written and evaluated, how presentations are delivered, how professional organizations are governed, and how colleagues from other parts of the country interact and collaborate.

While faculty introduces students to their disciplinary colleagues, they should allow students to bond with other graduate students who express similar interests in their discipline/field. Faculty co-presenting with individual students or a class of students socializes them further into the profession and models collegiality for them (Weidman, Twale, & Stein, 2001). Interesting graduate students in this aspect of the profession may also entice them to pursue administrative roles in these professional associations and conferences. Networking at conferences should also give students a jump-start on their career and enhance their job candidacy.

Involvement in conferences offers many positive professional opportunities. Conference presentations force students to expose their ideas to a larger professional audience, gain valuable constructive critique, take risks, and conquer fears (Shambaugh, 2000). Anderson (1996) recommended mandatory collaboration between faculty and students in grant proposal writing and conference proposal writing and presentation. By the same token, when faculty agrees to read

128

and evaluate conference proposals, they should consider introducing and involving advanced doctoral students in the process by also allowing students to evaluate them too. Subsequently, the chair and advisee(s) can compare and discuss their evaluations for consensus.

Supervising dissertations helps faculty build their own academic capital. Sweitzer (2009) contended that a faculty's professional identity can be enhanced by working with promising doctoral students. That investment grows with co-authored publications and presentations from the dissertation as well as student job placement and subsequent awards. On a cautionary note, academic capital may be jeopardized when faculty chairs controversial topics, oversees research of questionable value to the field/discipline, or validates marginal student work (Buraway, 2005).

RESEARCHING AND WRITING: COLLABORATION AND CO-AUTHORSHIP OF SCHOLARLY WORKS

Ideally, co-authorship follows a co-presentation of the research at a professional conference. Collaboration and co-authorship allow students to maneuver through the whole process and further integrate and socialize them for the profession (Weidman et al, 2001). How faculty advisors guide this writing process can range from exploitive or personal gain to mutually and professionally rewarding. The process may also be guided by discipline, demographics, and supervisory lines. For instance, men were more likely than women to co-author publications with their advisors (Tenenbaum, Crosby, & Gliner, 2001).

Co-authorship enhances faculty benefits associated with publishing (merit, promotion, tenure). It furthers the need to inculcate doctoral students into the research and publication process. Faculty supervisors/chairs should identify students and encourage them to do collaborative research to build their confidence with independent scholarship. Opportunities, however, arise in some fields (science) more easily than they do in other areas (humanities) (Maher, Timmerman, Feldon, & Strickland, 2013).

Any subsequent presentation or publication from the thesis/dissertation implies a certain degree of prestige and accomplishment on the part of the chair and committee members. The publishable outcomes begin a professional history the student and chair share. Impetus for prestige throughout that history will come from faculty chairs desiring the best from their protégées and ultimately encouraging and guiding them through the academic rites of passage (Isaac et al, 1992). However, while faculty eagerly touts the content of their scholarly writing they rarely, if ever, discuss the sometimes agonizing process of bringing their scholarship to realization.

Seldom do faculty share with master's/doctoral students *how* to write for a scholarly journal, how to select one journal over another, and what it takes to finally see the manuscript in print (Belcher, 2009). In an effort to not keep it a secret, Belcher suggested that prolific scholars may consider offering a team-facilitated scholarly article writing workshop. National and regional conferences should offer sessions on how to publish in their association-sponsored journals. More importantly, the easiest way to tell advisees to comprehend scholarly writing is to read it frequently in refereed journals in order to inculcate the technical and cognitive structure of the scholarly publishing format.

Manuscript Production

Getting a publication(s) from the dissertation can be trying for the newly minted scholar. Faculty should remind students that a dissertation is a dissertation, something not easily transitioned into a saleable book or a fountain from which many articles flow (Mulholland, 2011). Students need to think of the transition process as a new beginning rather than a simple thesis/dissertation revision (Belcher, 2009). Faculty need to know *how* to transition a thesis/dissertation to an acceptable book or journal manuscripts in order to assist students with the process (Dowling, Savron, & Graham, 2013). Chairs/committee members can inform graduates that the process means not blocking and moving paragraphs and sentences from the dissertation. Instead, rewriting for the intended audience increases the chance of the piece being accepted for publication. Note also that writing for scholarly audiences differs from writing for professional/practitioner audiences. A scholarly audience will expect to see well-chosen and presented research with results and discussion that flow from the data, while a practitioner audience will want to see an application of the findings useful to professional practice.

Faculty should instill confidence and encouragement in their advisees by offering their time and support throughout the writing process. Manuscript development for publication necessitates regular meeting times to work on drafts and meet deadlines. Faculty can digest the reviewers' comments with the student, contemplate revision and resubmission, offer proofreading services, and suggest revisions as well as provide a dry shoulder should the manuscript be rejected outright (Beatty, 2001; Brewer, Marmon, & McMahon-Landers, 2004).

Online tutorials can also help faculty and their advisees with publishing strategies that address information on the publication process, idea generation, finding a target audience and related journal home for the manuscript, and submission guidelines (Knievel, 2008). Faculty can also direct students to the campus writing center for further assistance (Di Pierro, 2007). Faculty should help students target journals whose audiences would best be served in reading the student's research study. An examination of the thesis/dissertation reference list may provide clues as to where the audience and journal outlet for the student's scholarship may lie (Beatty, 2001).

Deciding Authorship

Authorship Options

Eight students enrolled in Professor Rakoczy's doctoral seminar. He assigned students their basic term paper topic, which was his major research stream. His research area would be their dependent variable and they would each select a different independent variable to study. Near the end of the semester, Rakoczy informed the class that he had secured a contract for an edited book with a reputable academic publisher. He would pen the first and last chapters and their papers would be the other eight chapters. His name appeared on the book as the editor. Two pages in the beginning of the book would include their bios but they would not receive any royalties for the book. He asked them to sign a waiver prior to their finishing the course allowing him to use their papers. All agreed, but some more reluctantly than others. Simultaneously, eight different students enrolled in Professor Reed's doctoral cohort. They contracted in the beginning of the semester to write as their term project a co-authored paper they would submit to a scholarly journal for publication. They each contributed to the project including Reed. She collaborated with them on the topic, data gathering, editing, identifying several potential outlets for the piece, and drafting a cover letter to a journal editor. She asked how the students should be listed on the article. They felt she should be first; she disagreed. They decided they had collaborated well enough to list the names alphabetically with Reed listed last. They submitted the paper for publication and it was accepted.

Chairs and committee members should not demand or expect article co-authorship with students. Despite the American Psychological Association's (2002) ethical code, faculty and students still experience difficulty in assigning authorship to each other, fairly and equitably. To decrease confusion, faculty is advised to discuss co-authorship possibilities with students once they begin the research process as graduate research assistants, candidates for a degree, or students in a professor's class (Sandler & Russell, 2005). This discussion provides faculty and students in Reed's class extended opportunities to work together on a more equal basis (Whitley & Oddi, 1998). Perhaps a contract or consent form (an academic pre-nup) would be helpful especially given the real or perceived power differential that exists between faculty and students (Foster & Ray, 2012).

Costa and Gatz (1992) found that the degree of faculty input directly related to authorship. Because students differ in the type of faculty guidance they need, parties need a metric on how much input a faculty or student provides as a way to indicate order of authorship (Foster & Ray, 2012). Power differentials between faculty and students should not determine authorship credit but rather merit and work contributed should be the basis (Spiegal & Keith-Spiegel, 1970).

131

While there may be a prevailing norm that faculty receives second authorship as a *courtesy* on articles coming from a thesis/dissertation, most faculty do not support that norm. In some cases, faculty may assume a second authorship is forthcoming simply because they advised/supervised the student's work or they offered feedback. Professor Rakoczy expected first authorship because he came up with the topic although the students authored more of the piece (Foster & Ray, 2012).

Schiff and Ryan (1996) revealed that what some faculty viewed as unethical, other faculty regarded as normative within the field, which could explain why Rakoczy and Reed viewed the situation differently. Schiff and Ryan recommended faculty self-regulation. Foster and Ray's (2012) authorship model helps faculty and students determine the degree to which each involved themselves in idea development, completion of the tasks such as literature review, research process, amount of writing completed, draft revision, and overall quality and accuracy. When each party entered the process should also factor into the decision.

Rakoczy's soliciting student co-author waivers should have followed the close of the semester not before so as to diminish conflict of interest with student grades in the course. This was not an issue in Reed's class. University offices of research should consider drafting these types of contracts for faculty and students while also providing guidelines for uniform authorship credit.

Research Collaboration

Bonus Data

Professors Aoki and O'Connor collaborated together on research projects and also found themselves chairing and serving on the same two dissertation committees. In both cases, students Matt and Carol wished to conduct valuable university-wide research on undergraduates but the instrumentation each student needed exceeded their personal budgets. In both instances, Aoki and O'Connor approached the provost's office to underwrite the research by purchasing the instruments with the understanding that the students would provide the office with an executive summary of the results that would be of value to the university. In each case the instruments solicited more information than Matt and Carol needed to answer their research questions. Aoki and O'Connor contacted the provost's office and asked if they could use that leftover data for their own analyses and include the students in presentations and publications. All parties agreed. Subsequently, each student singly authored a conference presentation from their dissertation and co-authored two presentations and publications with Aoki and O'Connor. The provost's office received all deliverables.

The independent scholar notion should not connote isolation or the proverbial faculty silo (Buraway, 2005). At the graduate level, collaboration characterizes the PhD experience whether it be working with faculty on their research or completing the dissertation under faculty direction. The scope of collaboration within the department portends perhaps the degree to which the student will be exposed to and engaged with faculty in research projects. Disciplines and departments that are more collaboratively oriented are more likely to include and encourage their faculty to work collaboratively with graduate students as was Aoki and O'Connor's department. Wade-Benzoni, Roussseau, and Li (2006) suggested the formulating of a psychological contract to clarify and strengthen the faculty/student collaborative relationship. The contract should "include clearly stipulated expectations, a focus on research collaboration as opportunities or interaction, and structuring of tasks to provide the student with clear goals, and performance feedback" (p. 30). This opportunity allows students to participate more deeply in the professionalization process and prepare them for a future in academe or professional practice (Anderson, 1996; Weidman et al, 2001).

Austin and McDaniels (2006) recommended greater immersion in the research process which could be facilitated by clearer apprenticeship models where students follow more closely what faculty scholars are doing to satisfy their own research agenda. These could be modeled to students through grant writing, meeting IRB specifications, data collection and manuscript writing, and at conference presentations. Faculty must also model proper research behavior including ethical guidelines, full disclosure, and discussing the consequences of data falsification and plagiarism. Aoki and O'Connor showed Matt and Carol not only how to negotiate with administration but also found additional ways for them to positively view research. By collaborating with each other, they shared their research with colleagues and the university. This research moved students to greater levels of responsibility and self-discipline, and the team cooperation further helped them progress on their journey to independent scholars (McVey, Henderson, & Piercy, 2006).

New Publishing Options

Knowledge no longer comes just in bound, printed forms (Lang, 2002). Because dissertations can be produced electronically, faculty chairs need to not only know content but also know how to prepare students for new electronic mediums that could affect how and what constitutes a dissertation. University Microfilms International (UMI) accepts electronic dissertation submissions rather than hardbound copies in order to increase access to the information. Previous access through purchase or interlibrary loan meant that student work would not be freely available on the Internet.

Greater visibility of student work through electronic submission remains a benefit but it also raises concerns: Easy access may dissuade publication with a reputable scholarly publisher. Options now exist with regard to Internet access and faculty chairs and committees should assist students in deciding to allow or withhold dissemination of their thesis/dissertation in order to consider its market value as a unit in terms of future publication options rather than as scholarly article(s) (Lang, 2002).

FACULTY AND STUDENT START-UPS AND ENTREPRENEURIALISM

Entrepreneurial ventures would not be possible without human resources. Graduate students complete a portion of the scientific work through hard and soft money grants. While this certainly affords students beneficial career experiences and knowledge of scientific discovery, advisors must be cognizant of students' precarious positioning and vulnerability in terms of intellectual property rights, compensation, and exploitation of labor (Festel, 2013).

Faculty supervisors may collaborate with students entrepreneurially to produce start-up companies and spin-offs of faculty-developed ventures (Åstebro, Bazzazian, & Braguinsky, 2012). When participating in these ventures, faculty needs to apprise students of the implications of patents, intellectual property, university spin-offs, start-up companies, product discovery, commercialization, and entrepreneurship, and how it relates to their role as graduate student (Meyer, 2006). Graduate students focused on completing their thesis/dissertation research tend not to realize the risks and opportunities of transferring their work into viable spin-offs or start-ups (Jacoby, 2013), or how this might conflict with the academic goals of the institution (Festel, 2013). According to Meyer, the risk may boil down to "genuine entrepreneurial intent rather than the 'necessity' to become entrepreneurial given the lack of 'industrial demand' (as) the driving motivation of academic inventor-entrepreneur" (p. 509).

Supervisors/advisors through the apprenticeship model may also expose students to entrepreneurs and business/industry gurus who provide practical models of and input for their prospective ventures. In the midst of a community of encouragement, hands-on advising/supervising takes center stage (Miller, Walsh, Hollar, Rideout, & Pittman, 2011). Miller et al touted the higher retention rate among graduate students learning about technology transfer and noted the added bonus of team and interdisciplinary involvement increasing collaborative efforts. However, when faculty becomes entrepreneurial, it alters the department culture and mission, which may be further affected by business and industry collaboration in academe (McDougall & Powers, 2005). Consequently, this may affect the time faculty has to advise/supervise and may alter what they emphasize, share with, and model to the student. However, McDougall and Powers noted that students will benefit from the presence of higher-quality faculty associated with entrepreneurial ventures.

BEST PRACTICES

- Graduate schools and departments should offer campus seminars or capstone courses that focus on exam preparation, proposal overviews, and mock defenses.
- Encourage faculty/student collaborative teams to attend professional association conferences. Professional associations should offer workshops, seminars, and sessions on faculty/student research collaboration, co-authorship, and publication (Lovitts, 2001).
- Add more depth and comprehensiveness to the university-wide graduate student database by monitoring graduate degree progress. Include comprehensive exam results, committee composition, program extensions requested, successfully defended dissertations, co-authored articles and conference presentations, and job placements both in the aggregate and by demographics (Di Pierro, 2007).
- Devise a co-authorship contract. Form a small college- or university-wide review panel to conciliate/mediate co-authorship issues and research propriety (Goodyear, Crego, & Johnston, 1992).

RESOURCES

- *Publish Not Perish: The Art and Craft of Publishing in Scholarly Journals,* an online tutorial (www.publishnotperish.org (retrieved April 8, 2014)), can assist new faculty and graduate students in their publishing roles (Knievel, 2008).
- *The American Psychological Association Code of Conduct* (2002) and information on APA guidelines can be found at www.apa.org/ethics/code/index.aspx. For specifics regarding faculty/student authorship, scroll to www.apa.org/ethics/code/index.aspx?item=11 (retrieved April 9, 2014; see also APA (2002)).
- At www.abdsurvivalguide.com/ chairs will find access to a free monthly email newsletter for surviving in the All But Dissertation stage to share with their doctoral candidates (retrieved April 9, 2014).
- To gain more information about why students fail to finish their dissertation in a timely fashion, advisors can use the *Academic Procrastination Inventory.* Information is located at www.sjdm.org/dmidi/Procrastination_Assessment_Scale_for_Students.html (retrieved April 16, 2014) or by reading Ferraria (2000, 2003) and Solomon and Rothblum (1984).
- Universities contemplating assessing faculty advisors, chairs, and committee members can consult the *Academic Advising Survey Instrument* (Barnes, Chard, Wolfe, Stasson, & Williams, 2011).
- For more information on publishing through University Microfilms International (UMI), visit the ProQuest website at www.proquest.com/products-services/dissertations/ (retrieved April 18, 2014).

135

REFERENCES

American Psychological Association. (2002). Ethical principles of psychologists and code of conduct. *American Psychologist, 57*, 1060–1073.

Anderson, M. (1996). Collaboration, the doctoral experience, and the departmental environment. *Review of Higher Education, 19*, 305–326.

Arnkoff, D., Glass, C., & Robinson, A. (1992). Cognitive processes, anxiety, and performance on doctoral dissertation oral examinations. *Journal of Counseling Psychology, 39*, 382–388.

Åstebro, T., Bazzazian, N., & Braguinsky, S. (2012). Startups by recent university graduates and their faculty: Implications for university entrepreneurship policy. *Research Policy, 41*, 663–677.

Austin, A., & McDaniels, M. (2006). Preparing the professoriat of the future: Graduate student socialization for faculty roles. In J. Smart (Ed.), *Higher education handbook of theory and research*, Volume 21 (pp. 397–456). Dordrecht, Netherlands: Springer.

Barnes, B., Chard, L., Wolfe, E., Stasson, M., & Williams, E. (2011). An evaluation of the psychometric properties of the *Graduate Advisory Survey* for doctoral students. *International Journal of Doctoral Studies, 6*, 1–17.

Beatty, S. (2001). The doctoral supervisor–student relationship: Some American advice for success. *The Marketing Review, 2*, 205–217.

Belcher, W. (2009). Reflections on ten years of teaching writing for publication to graduate students and junior faculty. *Journal of Scholarly Publication, 40*, 184–200.

Bloom, B., Engehart, M., Furst, F., Hill, W., & Krathwohl, D. (Eds.) (1984). *Taxonomy of educational objectives. Book 1: Cognitive domain*. New York: Longman.

Brewer, E., Marmon, D., & McMahon-Landers, J. (2004). Basic advice for manuscript preparation for junior faculty members and graduate students. *College Student Journal, 38*, 16–22.

Brubaker, J., & Rudy, W. (1997). *Higher education in transition* (4th ed.). New Brunswick, NJ: Transaction Publishers.

Buraway, M. (2005). Combat in the dissertation zone. *American Sociologist, 36*(2), 42–56.

Church, S. (2009). Facing reality: What are doctoral students' chances for success? *Journal of Instructional Psychology, 36*, 307–316.

Costa, M., & Gatz, M. (1992). Determination of authorship credit in published dissertations. *Psychological Science, 3*, 354–357.

Damrosch, D. (1995). *We scholars: Changing the culture of the university.* Cambridge, MA: Harvard University Press.

Diamond, R. (1993). Changing priorities and the faculty reward system. In R. Diamond & B. Adam (Eds.), *Recognizing faculty work: Reward systems for the year 2000* (pp. 5–22). New Directions for Higher Education, no. 81. San Francisco: Jossey-Bass.

Di Pierro, M. (2007). Excellence in doctoral education: Defining best practices. *College Student Journal, 41*, 368–375.

Dowling, D., Savron, C., & Graham, G. (2013). Writing for publication: Perspectives of graduate nursing students and doctorally prepared faculty. *Journal of Nursing Education, 52*, 371–375.

Ferreira, M. (2000). *The ideal advisor: Graduate science students' perspective*. (ERIC Document Reproduction Service No. ED441 681)

Ferreira, M. (2003). Gender issues related to graduate student attrition in two science departments. *International Journal of Science in Education, 25*, 969–989.

Festel, G. (2013). Academic spin-offs, corporate spin-outs, and company internal start-ups as technology transfer approach. *Journal of Technology Transfer, 38*, 454–470.

Foster, R., & Ray, D. (2012). An ethical decision-making model to determine authorship credit in publishing faculty–student collaborations. *Counseling and Values, 57*, 214–239.

Freeman, D., & Loadman, W. (1985). Advice to doctoral guidance committees from alumni from two universities. *Research in Higher Education, 22*, 335–346.

Goodchild, L., & Miller, M. (1997). The American doctorate and dissertation: Six developmental stages. In L. Goodchild, K. Green, E. Katz, & R. Kluever (Eds.), *Rethinking the dissertation process: Tackling personal and institutional obstacles* (pp. 17–32). New Directions for Higher Education, no. 99. San Francisco: Jossey-Bass.

Goodyear, R., Crego, C., & Johnston, M. (1992). Ethical issues in the supervision of student researchers. *Professional Psychology: Research and Practice, 23*, 203–210.

Grabbe, L. (2003). The trials of being a PhD external examiner. *Quality Assurance in Education, 11*, 128–133.

Hartley, J., & Fox, C. (2004). Assessing the mock viva: The experiences of British doctoral students. *Studies in Higher Education, 29*, 727–738.

Isaac, P., Quinlan, S., & Walker, W. (1992). Faculty perspectives of the doctoral dissertation. *Journal of Higher Education, 63*, 241–268.

Jacoby, M. (2013). Students, start-ups, and bio-renewability. *Chemical and Engineering News, 91*(43), 33–35.

Knievel, J. (2008). Instructions to faculty and graduate students: A tutorial to teach publication strategies. *Portal: Libraries and the Academy, 8*, 175–186.

Krathwohl, D., Bloom, B., & Masia, B. (1964). *Taxonomy of educational objectives. Book 2: Affective domain*. New York: Longman.

Lang, S. (2002). Electronic dissertations: Preparing students for our past and their futures. *College English, 64*, 680–695.

Lovitts, B. (2001). *Leaving the ivory tower: The causes and consequences of departure from doctoral study*. Lanham, MD: Rowman-Littlefield.

Madsen, C. (2003). Instruction and supervision of graduate students in music education. *Research Studies in Education, 21*, 72–79.

Maher, M., Timmerman, B., Feldon, D., & Strickland, D. (2013). Factors affecting the occurrence of faculty–doctoral student co-authorship. *Journal of Higher Education, 84*, 121–143.

Mawn, B., & Goldberg, S. (2012). Trends in the nursing doctoral comprehensive examination process: A national survey. *Journal of Professional Nursing, 28*, 156–162.

McDougall, P., & Powers, J. (2005). University start-up formation and technology licensing with firms that go public: A resource-based view of academic entrepreneurship. *Journal of Business Venturing, 20*, 291–311.

McVey, L., Henderson, T., & Piercy, F. (2006). Cooperative learning through college faculty–student research teams. *Family Relations, 55*, 252–262.

Meyer, M. (2006). Academic inventiveness and entrepreneurship: On the importance of start-up companies in commercializing academic patents. *Journal of Technology Transfer, 31*, 501–510.

Miller, T., Walsh, S., Hollar, S., Rideout, E., & Pittman, B. (2011). Engineering and innovation: An immersion start-up experience. *Computer, 28*(4), 38–46.

Morris, M.C., Gallagher, T., & Ridgway, P. (2012). Tools used to assess medical student comprehensives in practical skills at the end of a primary medical degree: A systematic review. *Medical Education Online 17*, 18398.

Mulholland, J. (2011). What I've learned about revising a dissertation. *Journal of Scholarly Publishing, 43*, 39–51.

Nettles, M., & Millett, C. (2006). *Three magic letters: Getting the Ph.D.* Baltimore: Johns Hopkins University Press.

Parsons, T., & Platt, G. (1973). *The American university.* Cambridge, MA: Harvard University Press.

Pelfrey, W., & Hague, J. (2000). Examining the comprehensive examination: Meeting educational program objectives. *Journal of Criminal Justice Education, 11*, 167–178.

Sandler, J., & Russell, B. (2005). Faculty–student collaboration: Ethics and satisfaction in authorship credit. *Ethics and Behavior, 15*, 65–80.

Schiff, F., & Ryan, M. (1996). Ethical problems in advising theses and dissertations. *Journalism and Mass Communication Education, 51*, 23–36.

Shambaugh, R.N. (2000). Reframing doctoral programs: A program of human inquiry for doctoral students and faculty advisors. *Innovative Higher Education, 24*, 295–308.

Solomon, L., & Rothblum, E. (1984). Academic procrastination: Frequency and cognitive-behavioral correlates. *Journal of Counseling Psychology, 31*, 503–509.

Spiegel, D., & Keith-Spiegel, P. (1970). Assignment of publication credits: Ethics and practices of psychologists. *American Psychologist, 25*, 738–747.

Sweitzer, V. (2009). Towards a theory of doctoral student professional identity development. *Journal of Higher Education, 80*, 1–33.

Tenenbaum, H., Crosby, F., & Gliner, M. (2001). Mentoring relationships in graduate school. *Journal of Vocational Behavior, 59*, 326–341.

TWIG Writing Group. (1996). A feminist perspective on graduate student–advisor relationships. *Feminist Teacher, 10*, 17–25.

Wade-Benzoni, K., Rousseau, D., & Li, M. (2006). Managing relationships across generations of academics: Psychological contracts in faculty–doctoral student collaboration. *International Journal of Conflict Management*, *17*, 4–33.

Weidman, J., Twale, D., & Stein, E. (2001). *Socialization of graduate and professional students in higher education: A perilous passage?* San Francisco: Jossey-Bass.

Whitley, G., & Oddi, L. (1998). Graduate student–faculty collaboration in research and publication. *Western Journal of Nursing*, *20*, 572–583.

Chapter 10

Summarizing Best Practices

Articulating the faculty advising/chairing/supervising roles, chapter by chapter makes them seem even more complex and daunting. The research literature from the soft fields, the hard sciences, and the professions offered a vast array of information on these roles and also suggestions for improving them. Putting the bits and pieces of these researchers' recommendations together in one book may serve as the best gift a retiring professor can give to colleagues and subsequent generations of academics. Isolated in myriad articles, this collective wisdom shared across multiple fields and disciplines allows us to borrow from each other's experiences rather than continually re-invent ways to perform these roles.

Faculty and administrators should not only be talking about graduate advising but should also be aggregating data across campus to provide program directors and policy makers with more composite information on graduate student retention. Data can engage faculty to initiate disciplinary and interdisciplinary discussions about improving graduate advising, supervising, and thesis/dissertation chairing. Individually, graduate faculty must take time to self-evaluate all aspects of their advising/supervising/chairing roles and participate in professional development endeavors to ensure a higher quality of service. Researchers may find graduate advising/chairing/supervising an area ripe for further study.

Best practice themes are reconfigured here with the hope that program coordinators and directors, graduate deans, academic deans, provosts, professional associations, offsite supervisors, and faculty development officers realize the challenges graduate faculty face. These administrators play a role in assisting advisors/supervisors/chairs not only to achieve their own potential but also to improve graduate student experiences, satisfaction, and retention through continued research support and dissemination.

PLANNING AND DOCUMENTATION

Faculty along with their advisees should create an advising plan to facilitate goals and expectations. Faculty in conjunction with department chairs should create a plan to address workload expectations. Each party should discuss what each expects of the other in their role (Allen & Smith, 2008; Schlosser, Knox, Moskowitz, & Hill, 2003). Advisor/advisee should keep a log of all meetings and work sessions (Beatty, 2001).

QUALITY ADVISING THROUGH PROFESSIONAL DEVELOPMENT

Preparing future academics to advise is critical and should begin during graduate training rather than take place haphazardly on the job (Austin & McDaniels, 2006). Pair seasoned advisors/chairs with new faculty to serve on theses/dissertations (Cassuto, 2012; Knox, Schlosser, Pruitt, & Hill, 2006). Offer ongoing chair/advisor just-in-time, online professional development workshops (Di Pierro, 2007, 2013; Subramanian, Anderson, Morgaine, & Thompson, 2013) as well as face-to-face sessions at professional conferences (Titus & Ballou, 2013).

Advising/chairing/supervising *can* be measured. Existing instruments offer a framework that can prompt campuses to design instruments specific to an institution, field, or discipline (Golde & Dore, 2001; Harrison, 2012; O'Meara, Knudsen, & Jones, 2013; Schlosser & Gelso, 2001, 2005; Schlosser, Lyons, Talleyrand, Kim, & Johnson, 2011). Faculty should learn more about their own advisory/supervisory style, and their strengths and benefits in an effort to craft a more rounded advising/supervising style (Noy & Ray, 2012).

TAILORED AND CONSISTENT STANDARDS AND PRACTICES

Faculty tends not to thoroughly apprise applicants or newly admitted students of the rigors and goals of graduate education. Instead, much is left to chance, shrouded in mystery, and passed haphazardly from generation to generation and peer to peer like gossip or scuttlebutt (Heathcott, 2007; Lovitts, 2001). This can circumvent university or department policy and procedures and circulate timely, but potentially inaccurate information. Advisors/chairs/supersvisors must be open and immediate with advisee/supervisees (Barres, 2013; TWIG, 1996). Lovitts (2001) recommended faculty provide students with as much information as possible before entry, at entry, and throughout their program.

Faculty needs advising/supervising norms that maintain clear professional/business-like boundaries in the supervisor/supervisee, advisor/advisee, and chair/advisee relationships with regard to time, contact, communications, and expectations (Braxton, Proper, & Bayer, 2011; Knox et al, 2006; Rupert & Holmes, 1997). Faculty who internalizes the norms and acts in compliance with them models that to students and helps them internalize those norms (Braxton et al, 2011).

Departments need to enforce normative standards of behavior regarding advising, supervising, and chairing (Mieczkowski, 1995). Guidelines and policy for graduate advising/supervising/chairing responsibilities needs to be more explicitly stated and followed (Titus & Ballou, 2013). Better articulation of the role expectations for faculty advisor, supervisor, and chair are needed.

Working through the dissertation phase is where the student and faculty personalities reach greater work intimacy (Boyer, 1997; Holmes, 2002; Twale, 2007) therefore, workshops/seminars should be scheduled for advisors/chairs and advisees at each stage of the master's/doctoral program to address a variety of issues (Di Pierro, 2007). Maintaining a community of learners, community of scholars, or, where applicable, a community of practice should be considered.

DATA COLLECTION, AUDITS, EVALUATION, AND ASSESSMENT

Administrators must be cognizant as to how advising/supervising/chairing may be influenced, supported, or hampered as a result of the prevailing cultural, social, and political climate of a department or program (O'Meara et al, 2013). An audit of the department's climate should be considered. Juxtapose what the department and program *are* doing against a best practice model of what they *could/should* be doing as well as benchmark it with what they *did* in the past. Audits should include orientation opportunities; department policies and procedures related to program entrance through graduation; faculty vitae available to students; curriculum philosophy and options; available resources; expectations for coursework, comprehensive exams, and theses/dissertations; social activities instituted to facilitate faculty, student, and peer contact; and scholarly opportunities with faculty like sponsored research, entrepreneurial opportunities, conference presentations, and journal publication (Adams, 1993).

Students chose not to meet with their advisor or an administrator prior to or following their departure to illuminate difficulties or share concerns (Golde, 2000). Exit information is critically needed to resolve advising, administrative, organizational, cultural, climate, and/or academic issues related to student departure. This can separate matters over which the department has no control from those over which they do. Departments should perform student needs assessment and student evaluations of advisors/supervisors/chairs using instrumentation, focus groups, exit interviews, and benchmarking. Alumni can provide additional valuable information with less risk (Lovitts, 2001; Nesheim, 2006).

Results of the student evaluation of advisors/supervisors/chairs should be addressed in annual performance appraisal meetings.

Bair and Haworth (1999) acknowledged that systematic study of graduate schools and graduate programs especially in terms of student departure or persistence measures comes from the lack of comprehensive master's/doctoral data collection beyond admission, candidacy, or graduation. Bowen and Rudestine (1992) and Tuchman (2013) suggested that universities take as much interest in mining the graduate student data as they do in undergraduate data. Unfortunately, each graduate program within the university differs and, therefore, student admission information is not centralized but rather decentralized by school and department and perhaps programs within departments. As a result, aggregation and analysis of data may not be helpful. Data *would* be helpful to each unique individual program at each institution, but in all likelihood, not enough programs maintain complete records on every admitted student (*The Path to the PhD*, 1996). Administrators should consider information/data centralization to track graduate student recruitment, admission, retention, and graduation rates. Then, share this information with program coordinators and directors in order for them to make informed program decisions (Di Pierro, 2013; Tuchman, 2013). Furthermore, referencing specific program data with that published by the Council of Graduate Schools could be revealing (www.cgsnet.org, retrieved July 19, 2014). A closer look at the research may highlight the effects of graduate faculty advising/ supervising/chairing on retention.

MONITORING AND REWARDING GOOD ADVISING

Department chairs should consider better tracking or monitoring of graduate student advisor/supervisor/chair workloads. Note that online advising may be more time consuming than advising face to face. Department chairs and/or program directors/coordinators can keep records of advising loads, thereby avoiding overload by recognizing particularly heavy semesters. Advisors/chairs need to monitor how much time they spend with each student in relation to their overall workload (Barres, 2013; Di Pierro, 2013). Advising may become less time consuming but equally as effective by considering group/team/committee advising approaches, using social media, and forming learning communities.

Departments should offer incentives, rewards, and awards to acknowledge highly effective advisors/supervisors/chairs. This would encourage faculty to take an interest in overseeing graduate student research and dissertation committee work as well as to strengthen the advising and chair roles by giving them greater priority in the workload (Austin, 2002; Knox et al, 2006; Liechty, Schull, & Liao, 2009; Lovitts, 2008; Schlosser et al, 2011; Tierney, 1997; Titus & Ballou, 2013). Outstanding advisors/supervisors/chairs need to be professionally acknowledged annually, by adding an advising category along with teaching, research, and service awards.

ACKNOWLEDGING THAT LIFE HAPPENS

To minimize advisor/advisee and supervisor/supervisee differences, carefully match these dyads (Hilmer & Hilmer, 2009) especially given the diversity of students in graduate programs (Knox et al, 2006). However, faculty can expect occasional advising mismatches, nightmares, and disasters over their tenure mixed with a steady complement of productive graduate student relationships (Cassuto, 2012). Faculty should also be encouraged to promptly deal with matters rather than let them escalate. Faculty should maintain professional boundaries and use professionalism in decision-making. To ensure a level of quality, the number of each faculty member's advisees should be limited (Cassuto, 2012). Faculty must keep students on pace with their program considering advisees' abilities and time constraints, not pushing them too quickly or slowing their progress, not allowing them to skip important aspects of their program, or shortcut rites of passage in order to meet a university or personal deadline (Knox et al, 2006).

Finally, faculty needs to rethink the advising/supervising/chair roles differently to accommodate new student populations and new virtual ways of delivering graduate education and communicating with students. Traditional methods may still inform us but they should not limit us or our connection to graduate advisees/supervisees. Faculty priority should be overseeing and socializing graduate students for the future of higher education, not the past. The power faculty holds in the advisor/advisee relationship pales in comparison to the power advising has to mold the future of our disciplines and professions. Let's begin to use *that* power to transform our advising, supervising, and chairing duties to affect positively the next generation of scholar and practitioners.

REFERENCES

Adams, H. (1993). *Focusing on the campus milieu: A guide for enhancing the graduate school climate*. Notre Dame University: National Center for the Graduation of Minorities. (ERIC Document Reproduction Service No. ED381 065)

Allen, J., & Smith, C. (2008). Faculty and student perspectives on advising: Implications for student dissatisfaction. *Journal of College Student Development, 49*, 609–624.

Austin, A. (2002). Preparing the next generation of faculty: Graduate school as socialization to the academic career. *Journal of Higher Education, 73*, 94–122.

Austin, A., & McDaniels, M. (2006). Preparing the professoriat of the future: Graduate student socialization for faculty roles. In J. Smart (Ed.), *Higher education handbook of theory and research*, Volume 21 (pp. 397–456). Dordrecht, Netherlands: Springer.

Bair, C., & Haworth, J. (1999, November). *Doctoral student attrition and persistence: A meta-synthesis of research.* Paper presented at the annual meeting of the Association for the Study of Higher Education, San Antonio, TX. (ERIC Document Reproduction Service No. ED437 008)

Barres, B. (2013). How to pick a graduate advisor. *Neuron, 80,* 275–279.

Beatty, S. (2001). The doctoral supervisor–student relationship: Some American advice for success. *The Marketing Review, 2,* 205–217.

Bowen, H., & Rudenstine, N. (1992). *In pursuit of the PhD.* Princeton, NJ: Princeton University Press.

Boyer, E. (1997). *Scholarship reconsidered: Priorities of the professoriate.* San Francisco: Jossey-Bass.

Braxton, J., Proper, E., & Bayer, A. (2011). *Professors behaving badly.* Baltimore: Johns Hopkins University Press.

Cassuto, L. (Ed.) (2012). *Surviving your graduate school advisor.* Washington, DC: The Chronicle of Higher Education.

Di Pierro, M. (2007). Excellence in doctoral education: Defining best practices. *College Student Journal, 41,* 368–375.

Di Pierro, M. (2013). Strategies for doctoral student retention: Taking the roads less traveled. *Journal for Quality and Performance, 35*(3), 29–32.

Golde, C. (2000). Should I stay or should I go? Student descriptions of the doctoral attrition process. *Review of Higher Education, 23,* 199–227.

Golde, C., & Dore, T. (2001). *Survey of doctoral education and career preparation.* www.phd-survey.org/ (retrieved April 16, 2014).

Harrison, E. (2012). Development and pilot testing of a faculty advisor evaluation questionnaire. *Journal of Nursing Education, 51,* 167–169.

Heathcott, J. (2007). Blueprints, tools, and the reality before us: Improving doctoral education in the humanities. *Change, 39*(5), 46–51.

Hilmer, M., & Hilmer, C. (2009). Fishes, ponds, and productivity: Student–advisor matching and early career publication success for economic PhDs. *Economic Inquiry, 47,* 290–303.

Holmes, M.L. (2002). Why write a dissertation? In N. Welch, C. Latterell, C. Moore, & S. Carter-Tod, *The dissertation and the discipline* (pp. 119–125). Cross Currents: New Perspectives in Rhetoric and Composition. Portsmouth, NH: Boynton/Cook.

Knox, S., Schlosser, L., Pruitt, N., & Hill, C. (2006). A qualitative examination of graduate advising relationships: The advisor perspective. *Counseling Psychologist, 34,* 489–518.

Liechty, J., Schull, C., & Liao, M. (2009). Facilitating dissertation completion and success among doctoral students in social work. *Journal of Social Work Education, 45,* 481–498.

Lovitts, B. (2001). *Leaving the ivory tower: The causes and consequences of departure from doctoral study.* Lanham, MD: Rowman-Littlefield.

145

Lovitts, B. (2008). The transition to independent research: Who makes it, who doesn't, and why. *Journal of Higher Education, 79*, 295–325.

Mieczkowski, B. (1995). *The rot at the top: Dysfunctional bureaucracy in academe.* Lanham, MD: University Press of America.

Nesheim, B. (2006). If you want to know. In M. Guentzel & B. Neisham (Eds.), *Supporting graduate and professional students: The role of student affairs* (pp. 5–19). New Direction for Student Services no. 115. Hoboken, NJ: Wiley & Sons.

Noy, S., & Ray, R. (2012). Graduate student perceptions of their advisors: Is there systematic disadvantage in mentorship? *Journal of Higher Education, 83*, 876–914.

O'Meara, K., Knudsen, K., & Jones, J. (2013). The role of emotional competency in faculty–doctoral student relationships. *Review of Higher Education, 36*, 315–347.

Rupert, P., & Holmes, D. (1997). Dual relationships in higher education: Professional and institutional guidelines. *Journal of Higher Education, 68*, 660–678.

Schlosser, L., & Gelso, C. (2001). Measuring the working alliance in advisor–advisee relationships in graduate school. *Journal of Counseling Psychology, 48*, 157–167.

Schlosser, L., & Gelso, C. (2005). *The advisory working alliance inventory—advisor version:* Scale development and validation. *Journal of Counseling Psychology, 52*, 650–654.

Schlosser, L., Knox, S., Moskowitz, A., & Hill, C. (2003). A qualitative examination of graduate advising relationships: The advisee perspective. *Journal of Counseling Psychology, 50*, 178–188.

Schlosser, L., Lyons, H., Talleyrand, R., Kim, B., & Johnson, W.B. (2011). A multicultural infused model of graduate advising relationships. *Journal of Career Development, 38*, 44–61.

Subramanian, J., Anderson, V., Morgaine, K., & Thompson, W. (2013). Effective and ineffective supervision in postgraduate dental education: A qualitative study. *European Journal of Dental Education, 17*(1), e142–e150.

The path to the PhD: Measuring graduate attrition in science and humanities. (1996). Washington, DC: National Association of Science—National Research Council. (ERIC Document Reproduction Service No. ED420 536)

Tierney, W. (1997). Organizational socialization in higher education. *Journal of Higher Education, 68*, 1–16.

Titus, S., & Ballou, J. (2013). Faculty members' perceptions of advising versus mentoring: Does the name matter? *Science and Engineering Ethics, 19*, 1267–1281.

Tuchman, G. (2013). *Wannabe U: Inside the corporate university.* Chicago: University of Chicago Press.

Twale, D. (2007). Role of the dissertation. In D. Wright & M. Miller (Eds.), *Training higher education policy makers ad leaders: A graduate program perspective* (pp. 139–152). Charlotte, NC: Information Age Publishing.

TWIG Writing Group. (1996). A feminist perspective on graduate student–advisor relationships. *Feminist Teacher, 10*, 17–25.

Index

ABD (all but dissertation) status 8, 49, 98, 117, 135

Academic Advising Survey Instrument 135

academic capital 129

academic integrity 84–85

academic peer review 36

Academic Procrastination Inventory 135

access to faculty 1

Adams, H. 58

administrative advice 117–118

admissions: best practice 25; cognitive factors 17, 18, 19, 25; conditional 25; credential re-reviews 22; interviewing 19–20, 25; letters of recommendation 20; non-cognitive factors 17, 18–19, 20, 25; portfolio options 18–19, 23, 110; probability for student success 24; professional practice experience 20; re-interviewing 22; requirements and criteria 14, 17–20; writing samples 20

Adrian-Taylor, S. et al 79

advising: and attrition 4–5; distinguished from mentoring 9–10; monitoring and rewarding 143–144; outcomes, measuring 117; plans 103; as retention strategy 6–7; and rites of passage 7–9, 124–135; standards 23; style 110; teams 68, 99, 103

advisor/advisee relationship: assistance 47; best practice 52; communication 44, 50, 100–101; conflict 5, 144; cross-gender relationships 49, 52; cross-race relationships 49, 52; defining 43–46; and department climate 50; diverse groupings 48–49; doctoral vs master's students 42–43; evaluations 51–52; and faculty interests 52; feedback 45, 47; formalized administrative mechanisms 52; good advising 47; group/cohort seminars 52; honesty 45; interaction blogs 99, 101, 102, 103, 104; and international students 65–66, 88; and the laissez-fair advisor 49; matching and assignment 4, 21, 23–25, 52, 144; meetings 49, 52; mismatches 24, 144; poor advisors 49–50; preparation for 52; reciprocity 44; sustaining the dyad 46; trust 45; and the unpredictable advisor 49

advisors 47; in adversarial roles 46; as affective therapists 43; attitude 14; as available timely communicators 44; benefits and costs of 47–48; demeanor 49–50; evaluation 51–52; as exploitative users 43, 44; function 47; as instrumental advocates 43; as intellectual researchers 43–44; laissez-faire 49; monitoring 103; paternalistic 49; and respect 44, 47; role characterization 65, 110–111, 144;